The unauthorized reproduction or distribution of a copyrighted work is illegal. Criminal copyright infringement, including infringement without monetary gain, is investigated by the FBI and is punishable by fines and federal imprisonment.

Please purchase only authorized electronic editions and do not participate in or encourage, the electronic piracy of copyrighted. Your support of author's rights is appreciated.

This book is a work of fiction. Names, characters, places and incidents are the products of the author's imagination or used fictitiously. Any resemblance to actual events, locales or persons, living or dead is entirely coincidental.

Advance copyrighted 2021 by Delta James

Cover Design by: Dar Albert of Wicked Smart Designs

❋ Created with Vellum

ADVANCE

MASTERS OF THE SAVOY

DELTA JAMES

CHAPTER 1

*T*he next two days were spent wrapped in the sensual cocoon Fergus wove around me. Over and over again, he reached for me, drawing me under him before mounting me and tapping into my deeply hedonistic nature. Several times, I had been confronted by the alpha knot at the base of his cock, but each time he had suppressed it. It was an angry, fearsome thing, and I knew if he forced it inside me, I would be split asunder.

I was sleeping, sprawled across his body, when he maneuvered me onto my back, growling low and seductively. My body had come to respond in a very visceral way. Fergus's mouth descended onto mine, capturing it as he surged forward. I was unprepared for the sharp pain as the strength of his thrust forced the unsuppressed knot up inside me. I screamed into his mouth as my pussy tightened around him in a new way.

He held me tight, preventing evasion on my part, then stilled. My pussy clamped down as he kissed me and murmured words of love and encouragement. How could he talk of love to me? I feared I had lost myself to him, wanting to believe, but I knew better. I was merely one of the spoils of war. My sheath began to relax and accommodate his knot…

The buzzer from the front gate to her rambling mansion on North Carolina's Outer Banks interrupted her stream of free-flowing writing.

"Shit!" she groaned, picking up her cell phone and pulling up her security system's app.

Her publisher, Gail Vincent, was looking in the camera with a pinched look on her face. Gail often had a sour expression. She glanced at the antique mantle clock on her desk. *And shit again!* It was only eight in the morning.

They'd been together a long time. It had been Gail who had given Sage her first big break and taught her the ropes of becoming an author. Gail who had often believed in her when she didn't believe in herself. The relationship had changed as Sage had become more confident and more successful and no longer relied as heavily on Gail's advice.

Sage Matthews answered her cell, an embarrassed smile on her face. "Hi, Gail. Uhm… I'm not ready."

"I figured." Gail fussed, not able to hide the roll of her eyes. "That's why I came early. Did you look at the things I sent over?"

"Well, uhm, no…"

"For God's sake, Sage, open the damn gate. You seriously need a keeper—someone who stays out here and takes care of you."

"I have a housekeeper. Selma comes in once a week with her husband, Jerry. She cleans the inside while he does the outside," she said, pressing the button that would open the gate.

"Why on earth did you have to move to the middle of fucking nowhere? Why not stay in D.C., maybe get a place in Georgetown? Or Chicago? You always like it when we go to Chicago. Better yet, a nice loft in New York, maybe either in SoHo or Tribeca."

"I like my house, Gail. It's quiet, I can ramble around, and if I want to play music and dance around naked at three in the morning, there's no one to tell me no. I even have a private beach."

"That you won't let me take advantage of and throw an exclusive party. If you're going to have the damn thing, you should at least make use of it for your business. On my way…" Gail said as she drove her rented Mercedes up the drive.

Sage saved her paranormal novel and pulled up the latest Roark Samuels.

They were back in the beach cottage in Monaco. There

were no more kidnappers or assassins... just Melinda in a summery dress outside the glittering international Mecca known as Monte Carlo. Earlier in the day, Roark Samuels had killed the two assassins sent to dispose of the beautiful heiress. It was time she learned the consequences of not following orders... specifically his. Roark grabbed her by the wrist and yanked her over his muscular thighs. Pinning her in place with one hand, he pressed her shoulder blades down. Using his other, he rucked up the light, flimsy summer frock she was wearing, then caressed her shapely, ivory bottom.

Raising his hand, he brought it crashing down on her upturned backside. Melinda yowled and cursed at him, but Roark was enjoying what he was quite certain was a long, overdue punishment for her actions. Over and over, he spanked her rapidly-coloring globes and could feel her cool skin beginning to heat from his harsh strikes.

"Such a pretty bottom. Shame it has to get turned a bright shade of red because you couldn't do what you were told. When I get done with your spanking, it's going to feel really good when I'm pumping my hips into it as I give you a good, hard fucking."

"Roark, you sonofabitch, let me go!" she cried.

"Now, now, Melinda. Good girls accept their punishment when they've been naughty. Running away from home, then getting us into this situation, definitely qualifies as naughty."

With that admonishment, Roark continued to inflict a considerable amount of pain across her backside. Silence, except for the sound of his hand spanking her ass and the constant roar of the surf outside, filled the room. The longer and harder he spanked her, the stiffer his cock became. Melinda needed this spanking almost as much as he needed to give it to her.

"You think you can apologize to me and behave yourself?"

"Yes, please stop, Roark. I'm sorry," she said meekly.

He smiled. The sound of a woman's submission was sweet. He rubbed her reddened globes to acknowledge her acceptance of his dominance. When she tried to rise, he fisted her hair, dragging her up and bending her over the end of the bed he'd been sitting on. Without another word, he unfastened his pants and allowed his cock to jut away from his groin through the open fly. Stepping behind her, he spread her legs.

Roark guided his cock to her sheath before thrusting forward ferociously, forcing himself deep within her core and extracting a powerful climax from her. He grunted with satisfaction. He held her in place, wrapping one hand tightly around her hip and using the other to grasp the nape of her neck to press her down into the mattress as he took long, deep strokes.

Each time he drew back, the loss of being buried in her wet heat made him crave plunging back into her depths. Each time he drove forward, he swore he could feel the end of her sheath with the head of his shaft. He knew there was no escape for her from his relentless thrusting. He needed her to accept he was the one doing the fucking, and she was the one being fucked.

Roark's cock stroked her over and over as he grunted and

groaned in feral and primal satisfaction. Her body convulsed, her pussy contracting all along his length in the same rhythm that stroked her heated channel. He could feel her capitulation to his pleasure as well as to his dominance.

"Come for me!" he bellowed like an enraged bull as he thrust in and out.

She screamed his name as she toppled over the edge of ecstasy. He thrust into her three more times before his cock erupted, emptying his essence into her. When he was finished, he withdrew, his cock dripping the last of his seed.

Jesus, Roark, you're such a bastard, thought Sage.

Roark Samuels was the romantic hero of Sage's wildly popular erotic suspense series. The first book had been meant to be a standalone novel. When it shot to the top of all the best seller lists, her publisher, Gail Vincent, demanded she make it into a series. Now, her readers wouldn't allow her to bring it to an end.

She often remarked she spent more time with Roark than with anyone else. The success of the novels wasn't all sunshine and lollipops. The better they sold, the higher the demand, which had taken its toll on her personal life. *It was odd how some of the very best things in life grew out of the worst.*

Sage had been working for a conservative D.C. law firm and had a perfectly lovely fiancé and future all planned out. The problem came when she began reading erotic romance books. Some of them were wonderful—putting her in touch with a side of herself she'd never known and giving wing to her fantasies. Others had been severely lacking in both the quality of the writing and the editing.

She'd written her first novel on a lark and been shocked and thrilled when it had done well. Thinking it might be an excellent source of income to pay for their wedding, Sage had taken on her new hobby with a vengeance, spending copious amounts of time writing—often to the detriment of her relationship with her former fiancé, Derek. In retrospect, it was easy to see why when she'd been asked to leave the law firm, Derek had cited the same reasons, that he felt they would both do better if they called off their engagement.

John Quillen, the managing partner with the firm, had held up one of her novels as he'd faced her from across his desk.

"Is this your book?" he'd asked, staring down his nose at her. Sage had nodded. "Then I feel, Ms. Matthews that the firm has no choice but to ask for your resignation."

"But why? I didn't portray the firm in an unkind light. In fact, the book doesn't even have a single lawyer in it."

"Nevertheless, there are those who know you wrote it..."

Sensing there would be no way to dissuade them, Sage had said, "Well of course they do, my name is right there on the cover."

"Apparently you do not see how this kind of smut reflects poorly on the firm. You may resign and we will provide you an adequate reference or we will terminate your employment

and will not comment at all on your tenure here when future employers call asking for a reference. I'm sure you realize that no reference carries almost the same stigma as a bad one."

"I'll pack my things and leave my resignation on my desk."

And

"They fired you?" asked Derek when he'd arrived home in the townhouse they'd shared. "Good God, Sage, I warned you. We stretched to afford to buy this place. I damn near wiped out my savings for the down payment. We can't afford for you to be out of work."

"I know. I didn't mean for it to happen, and Gail thinks I could probably be making more if I had more time to write. I was going to talk to you about it after the wedding."

Derek had leaned over and said, "Look I thought it was a bit of a lark and would help bring in some extra money, but I warned you it was best to have a pen name. I never thought the damn thing would actually become a best seller."

She'd reached across the dinner table to place her hand over his. Derek had drawn back, placing both of his hands in his lap.

He continued, "Maybe we ought to take a break and rethink what we both want for our future."

His cold demeanor had rocked her back harder than her dismissal from the law firm. Truth to tell, there had been a part of her that had been excited to give the full-time author thing a try.

"A break? As in postponing the wedding?" Derek had nodded. "Are you planning to move out?"

"No, I paid most of the down payment. I can dip into my retirement to buy your interest out."

"So," Sage said narrowing her eyes and beginning to grasp the true enormity of the day's events, "you don't want to postpone the wedding, you want to call it off and kick me out."

"I wouldn't put it like that…"

"Of course you wouldn't. Not to worry Derek, I'll have my things packed and be gone before you get home tomorrow. If I don't have my share of the down payment wired to my account by the end of the day, you'll hear from my attorney and I will come after you for breach of promise, the townhouse and anything else he can think of."

"There's no need to get vindictive, Sage."

"I disagree. I think there's every reason." She stood up from the dinner table. *"I think you should go to a hotel tonight. I'll get started packing and will be gone from your life by this time tomorrow."*

"You might be right. I wish you well, Sage."

"Get out, Derek. I'm glad I found out what a cowardly bastard you were before I married you."

He'd thrown a few things in his overnight bag and had exited her townhouse and her life within thirty minutes.

Sage had called a friend who was on an extended cruise and arranged to borrow her home for a few weeks. Lydia lived in Charlotte, North Carolina, and Sage found the Southern charm, hospitality and lower cost of living was like a balm to her soul. Derek had repaid her portion of the down payment plus interest and half of what they'd paid on joint purchases for their home. She'd wanted to throw it back in his face, but her more practical nature took over.

Looking to start anew, Sage had begun scouring the real estate ads for the Outer Banks of the Carolinas. If she was going to build a new life, she would do it in a place she loved to be. Over the years she had remodeled not only the house but her very existence. Her author persona had become far removed from who she really was, but the façade of the successful writer paid the bills, it had allowed her to renovate the rambling mansion on the Outer Banks of North Carolina and pay off the mortgage. She was seen as a hard-driving, dominant woman who lived alone and liked it that way—yet nothing could have been further from the truth.

Sage laughed as she read the next to the last scene, taking a sip of Diet Coke and popping a piece of caramel corn in her mouth. Standing, she stretched, then trotted out of what had once been a solarium when her home had been built in the late 1800s. It was one of the first remodeling projects she'd taken on, much to her contractor's dismay. Sage had converted it into her office and had all the glass replaced with glass that could withstand a hurricane. Not only did Sage love to write there when the sky above was clear and sunny with billowy clouds overhead, but she adored it even more when the weather was dark and stormy. But then, Sage was something of a storm child.

"Hey, Gail!" she said, entering the foyer just as Gail stomped in.

"Please tell me you took a shower and washed your hair…"

Sage shook her head and grinned. "Nice to see you, too."

"For God's sake, Sage, you have a signing at the Huntington. We need to get there and get you set up."

"The signing isn't until tomorrow. I'll get up early in the morning…"

"Do you even read the attachments to the emails I send you?"

"I read the emails," Sage said sheepishly.

Gail rolled her eyes again. "There is a reception this evening, then you're hosting a Meet the Author breakfast, you have a panel with some of the other more notable authors, lunch, then the VIP signing, followed by the regular one. You need to get dressed in something presentable," Gail said as she steered Sage up the grand staircase toward the master bedroom.

"How about if you take the books and swag now? I'll get dressed and drive in by myself. You always like it when I make an entrance with the roadster."

Gail nodded, and Sage sensed she might be able to avoid a seven-hour tirade about how awful North Carolina was and how ungrateful Sage was for all Gail did. The fact was, Sage was grateful, but always kept in mind Gail was well paid for her services. She had long ago come to the conclusion that Gail was over-stressed and a complete control freak. Since most of the time that worked in Sage's favor, she usually just put up with it.

In the beginning and not knowing what to do, she had depended on Gail for just about everything. When she and Derek had split, Gail had gone to work ensuring that Sage would have a successful career as a writer. Gail had been willing to bet on her future success, figuratively and literally-often loaning Sage money or allowing her bill to slide for a month or two.

It wasn't that she wasn't grateful for all Gail had done; it was just that Gail had wanted her to continue to do the same thing and saw no need for change or to continue to advance her career past a certain level. Sage had disagreed and increasingly found herself in conflict with Gail.

"I promise to be there by six-thirty, then I'll change in the room. I'll even let you pick out my clothing for the event."

"Who the hell else would do it? You really need

a personal assistant—someone to run your schedule, pack for you, make appointments, run errands, etc."

"I like living alone," Sage said quietly.

Gail stopped and put a hand on her arm. "I know Derek leaving you was a shock. I hope he realizes what an idiot he was. Leaving before he married you and you made it big was just stupid."

"I'd like to think he would have married me because he loved me, not just for the possible divorce settlement, but I guess I have to appreciate that he recognized he couldn't handle it and broke it off."

"Appreciate?" Gail snorted. "The little weasel got embarrassed…"

"My books aren't for everybody, Gail, and I respect that. In any event, I have all the books and swag ready to go."

"Fine. It's probably better if you just swoop in. That ought to intimidate the other authors…"

"I don't want to intimidate people…"

"Why ever not? It allows you to command respect and kowtowing from the hotel, and it lends to your aura as the fabulous and slightly mysterious romance author." Gail made short work of packing her clothing. "I'm going to leave your makeup here and arrange for someone to get you ready for tonight and in the morning."

Eight hours later, Sage pulled up to the hotel in her vintage Rolls Royce roadster at precisely six-thirty. It had been her big splurge when her first Roark Samuels novel had hit big. The antique mansion was the second. It was a good thing they continued to sell well since both were damned expensive to keep up.

The concierge rushed out to greet her. "Ms. Matthews, how lovely to see you again. Ms. Vincent told us to expect you. Can I have your car parked and show you to your room?"

"Thank you so much," she said. Sage turned on a brilliant smile and waved as she walked over to the small crowd of readers who had gathered.

"Hi, guys! I have to run up to my room to get ready for the party, but I'm happy to sign anything you want when I come back down and during or after the party."

"Sage? Is Roark ever going to fall in love… really in love?" called one.

"Yeah, Roark needs his own happily ever after," said another.

"I'm not sure Roark knows anything about love other than how to spell it, although it isn't his favorite four-letter word. See y'all later," she called as the concierge bustled her inside and accompanied her to her suite on the ground level.

Gail met her at the door and ushered her inside, closing the door in the concierge's face.

"Gail, that was rude," Sage said quietly.

"The concierge is fine, and we need to get you ready. I got here early enough to pick up something for each of us for tonight. I found you the most beautiful LBD…"

"LBD?"

"Little Black Dress. It will be very slimming. Then, when I thought about what I brought, they would have clashed in style, so I picked up something for me."

Sage hid a knowing smile. Gail often found ways to justify Sage picking up the tab for something she wanted for herself. Sage allowed herself to be led to where the makeup artist and hairstylist were waiting and sat so they could begin their work.

"I'm going to lay out your dress and accessories. I have a key to your suite, so you won't need anything. I've arranged for them to run a tab for you all weekend, so all you need to do is sign. I don't want you to have to carry anything with you. You're so awkward when you try to manage a cocktail clutch and anything else."

"Thanks, Gail. You go on. I'll be fine, and I promise to be on time."

"Not on time, Sage, thirty minutes late." Gail leaned over and whispered in her ear, "I've arranged for one of the cover models to wait for you outside the door to be your plus one at the party. He's promised to be most attentive."

Sage rolled her eyes. *I wonder what that's going to set me back?* Gail often spent Sage's money like water through a sieve, but Gail's publicity and marketing had been an integral part of the success of the novels. So usually, Sage just took a deep breath and paid the bills.

As requested, Sage was thirty minutes late and smiled when she saw the model. Terrance had never graced the cover of one of her novels, but over the years they had become friends. Oddly, Roark had always been an illustration as opposed to a photo.

"Hey, Sage," he said, taking her arm and leaning down to kiss her cheek.

"Terrance, it's good to see you. How's Max?"

"He's great. We really enjoyed the murder mystery train tickets."

"Oh, good. I thought you might. I know it's kind of geeky…"

"And we're your favorite nerdy gay couple," he laughed.

Terrance was good company, and Sage was glad that if Gail felt she had to have arm candy, she had at least picked someone enjoyable.

They entered the party, which was already in full swing. As these things went, it was well organized and pretty swanky. Everyone was dressed to the nines, although no formal wear. Hotel staff had been pressed into service, not only serving drinks and hors d'oeuvres but staffing a table at the back where a selection of the attending authors' books was set up and being sold.

"It looks like only four of us have books available," Sage said.

Terrance laughed. "Only those of you who sponsored the party have books available. Honestly, Sage, do you even pay attention to what Gail signs you up for?"

"Not really."

She and Terrance mingled with the throng of admirers. This was Sage's second favorite part of being a successful author. Unlike for many authors who were painfully shy introverts, signing events were Sage's crack cocaine. She absolutely loved connecting with her readers on a personal level. Her favorite was the messages from readers about how her work had touched them, inspired them, entertained them. Knowing there were those who appreciated, even treasured what she did, made the doing all that much sweeter, and what it had cost her—a fiancé, a job, friends—was worth it.

Gail shouldered her way through the crowd gathered around her and Terrance.

"Sweetie, there's a few people I need you to meet," she said to Sage, leading her away.

Sage turned back to those who had books and

pens in their hands. "I'll be back and stay as long as you want me to sign your books. You can ogle Terrance all you want, but no touching."

Terrance grinned at her and was quickly surrounded.

"I don't know why you bother with those people…"

"Because they buy my books, because they took their hard-earned money and time to attend this event, and because without them, I wouldn't be able to make a living doing something I love."

Sage spent the next two hours rubbing elbows with some of the elite of the publishing world. Gail wanted to expand her readership beyond erotic romance and was even shopping one of her ideas around for a movie. There was a touch on her shoulder, and she spun around, the color leaving her face.

"Hello, Sage." She recognized Derek's voice.

"Derek. I'm surprised to see you," she said, keeping her voice devoid of emotion.

"You look good."

"I've gained some weight. You look great."

He really did, but then he always did. He woke up looking perfect. All he had to do was run his hands through his perfectly cut hair and it fell into place—unlike hers, which looked as if she'd just gotten laid… not that that was necessarily a bad look.

He leaned forward, kissing her cheek. Sage was relieved to realize that not only did it not hurt, it was oddly devoid of emotion. She was finally over him. She had gone from love to hate and now finally, to apathy.

"Given why you broke things off between us, I'm surprised to see you here."

"Well, Gwen actually rather enjoys these kinds of events. One of our clients has acquired a small studio and is talking to Gail about one of your books being made into a movie... one of the earlier books before they got so smutty."

Zing! He couldn't help himself... neither could she.

"Doesn't Gwen read the smutty ones?" asked Sage, feigning innocence.

Zing! Bullseye, she thought as he blushed. Hmm, Roark would never blush. She wondered if she could even embarrass a man like Roark. She didn't actually know any men like Roark, but she was quite certain that they didn't blush.

She was glad to see she'd hit her mark. His girlfriend, Gwen, was an avid reader and participant in her private reader group on Facebook. Gwen was also a lawyer and on track for partner, which she guessed was the real reason Derek had broken things off between them. There was a part of her that knew she should feel bad about being a bit bitchy, but this was her party, and she wasn't going to take crap from her ex.

She allowed Gail to move her through those she wanted Sage to meet, whispering in her ear who each person was and why they were important.

"Cindy Sellers, huge erotic romance blog. Always features our books and gives them stellar ratings on Goodreads, Bookbub, and all the retail platforms" Gail whispered. "Named you erotic romance writer of the year."

"Cindy! It's so good to see you. I can't thank you enough for all your support… and for naming me Erotic Romance Author of the Year. I was so touched."

"My pleasure, Sage, and I totally meant it. The bottle of wine was so sweet and so like you."

She'd have to remember to thank Gail for that.

Finally, the party started to die down and she looked for Terrance, who was surrounded by those who had waited. Sage hailed one of the servers.

"Ms. Matthews?" she said. "I just love your books."

"Thank you. I appreciate that. If there's one you'd like in paperback, just go grab it and I'll sign it for you."

"Really? Thanks! Now, what did you need?"

"See that group of readers with Terrance? Could you get their drink orders? See if you could also snag us a tray of hors d'oeuvres and put it on my tab?"

"I can do that. That's so sweet of you. You're not like most of them. You really seem to like your readers."

"I don't like my readers… I adore them. Join us if you can."

The server glanced at her watch. "I can do that. My shift just ended. I'll get you…"

"Us."

The girl's smile broadened. "Us set up."

Two hours later, the room was empty except for Sage, Terrance, and the last of the readers. When she'd signed the last book and received the last hug, they left the ballroom.

"Terrance, I'm going to take a stroll outside. It's really a lovely night."

"Want some company?"

"No, you go upstairs to Max and give him my love."

Terrance grinned, held up the wine bottle Sage had pressed into his hands, and left. She waved off the concierge and headed outside to one of the hotel's courtyards.

Pew! Snap! Pew! Snap!

Sage heard the sounds as pieces of bark from a nearby tree flew into her face. She dropped and rolled as another two bullets skimmed past where she had just been standing and embedded themselves in the tree. Rolling away, she got to her feet behind a dense cluster of bushes and ran toward the main hotel, screaming her head off.

The next sounds she heard were the tromping of footsteps and shouts of security people. Sage was hustled inside via a side door and immediately surrounded by hotel personnel who assured her that she was safe, and that the police had been called.

"Gail…" she started, realizing she was in shock.

"Sage, oh my God, Sage! I'm right here." Gail rushed to her side.

Thank God was right. Thank God for Gail, who swiftly took control of the situation and helped her file reports with the police, ensured her room was secured, asked the hotel to station additional security in and around Sage's suite, then helped Sage back to her room.

"Are you sure you're all right? Do you want me to order room service? The kitchen was about to close, but they said they'd be happy to make something to send up to you," Gail offered.

"That would be great. If I could get a big bowl of their cream of crab soup, a loaf of that bread they serve with lots of butter, and a couple of diet cokes, I would be so appreciative."

Gail ordered room service and stayed while Sage changed into her robe and the food arrived.

"If you're sure you don't need anything else…"

"No, thanks, Gail. I really appreciate it. I think I

might have been in shock. I don't really recall much of what happened."

"These local yokels aren't all that sure. They think probably kids out doing a bit of night shooting mistook you for something else. One idiot thinks someone was shooting at you."

"At me? Why would anyone want to shoot at me?"

"Who knows? I think things are probably so boring around here, he's just trying to make up something exciting. I'm sure it was just a couple of kids being stupid…"

The fog from the fear seemed to be dissipating. "But why would kids be shooting pistols with silencers in the dark?"

"What makes you think they had silencers?" asked Gail.

"There was no actual sound of a gunshot… you know, like a bang or the backfire of a car. All I heard was a kind of a weird spitting sound and pieces of the tree being chipped off by the bullets."

Gail laughed. "Who knows what silliness kids will get up to. They probably scared themselves more than you. Go easy on the bread and butter, will you?"

"Sure." Sage rolled her eyes. "Thanks again," she said, following Gail to the door and securing the night latch before double-checking the door that led to the private terrace.

She sat at the table and enjoyed her meal, devouring every bit of bread and dollop of butter. Heaven.

After she finished, she checked the doors again, then headed into the bath. She turned on the shower before getting out of her robe and taking a critical look at her body. She really did need to lose a few pounds, but hot artisan bread and butter was something not to be missed. Her relationship with food wasn't always healthy. Many times, she used it to comfort or soothe some part of herself, but she did try to keep an eye on her weight. Besides, someone had tried to shoot her, regardless of whether they thought she was some kind of varmint. She deserved a little indulgence.

CHAPTER 2

Sage stepped into the hot, pulsing shower and let the water rush over her. She adjusted the showerhead so it pounded against her tense muscles, forcing them to relax. Turning her back, the hot water did a lot to dispel not only the tension she had been holding in her body, but in her mind. She could feel everything beginning to unwind. By the time she got out, her good mood had been restored, her fears abated, and a feeling of sexiness began to creep over her body like the mist rolling in from the sea.

She walked back into the main suite and set up her laptop. Sage hadn't really planned on doing any writing while she was here, but she rarely went anywhere without her computer. She never knew when any new character might speak to her or when Roark had a new story to tell her. That was the oddest thing about her work—she wasn't a plotter who did meticulous research and planned out the entire book. She heard characters in her head, and she simply wrote down the stories they told her. No one understood the strength of Roark's personality.

Roark had started off as a fairly typical romantic hero, but from the beginning, she'd had trouble keeping him from going dark and just a bit kinky. The sex became more graphic in the second novel, which outsold the first almost two to one. By the fourth novel, he had begun spanking his heroine of the month and incorporating other elements of dominance and submission. Each novel did better than the ones before, so Gail insisted she continued to write them.

Sage had to admit, in the beginning, they had been fun to write, but more and more, she longed to do something else—paranormal, cowboy, romantic comedy, anything other than what she felt had become formulaic—but the money was too good to walk away from.

Flipping her laptop open, she sat in the comfortable office-style chair.

Let's see… where did I leave Roark… right, he'd just spanked and fucked his latest heroine…

He watched her as she worked. She was really quite lovely. Granted, she was not the size of a fashion model, but he'd never been particularly fond of skinny girls who looked like a teenage boy from the back. No, he wanted a woman with dangerous curves—voluptuous, with large breasts, and a smaller waist that flowed smoothly into generous hips. If she had a nice, luscious ass... all the better. Sage had been a bit on the thin side when they'd begun and always wore those severe suits with boring, serviceable lingerie. Now, she indulged herself, enjoyed life more, and her clothing was more in keeping with that of a successful romance writer. He wondered if people knew her fondness for expensive, utterly feminine lingerie and corsets. He liked it best when she danced around naked in the solarium.

Sage wrote for several hours, and finally, realizing the time, hit save on the story, turned off the light, removed her robe, and climbed into bed. She arranged the pillows so she was comfortable and didn't draw the covers over her body. He watched as she ran her hands down her body, glad she had worked on a sex scene—they often left her aroused and ready to play.

She moved her hands down to her mons, trailing down to part her labia and bring some of her honeyed moisture from her slit back up to her clit. Sage moaned and her toes curled, her legs relaxing to give her more room to pleasure herself. He wondered if she had any idea how incredibly desirable she was.

She rubbed her swollen nubbin in small circles with her index finger, using her other hand to separate the petals of her sex, isolating her clit, and exposing her pussy. God he loved looking at her pussy. The physical effects of her arousal could be seen—nipples stiff and hard, pussy soft and wet, and skin flushed with desire.

Sage reached into the bedside table. That naughty little minx—she'd packed her favorite vibrator. She stimulated her pleasure nub until it peeked out from under its hood, her breath becoming thready. Setting the toy to a lovely hum, she placed it against her clit and let it work its magic while her other hand went up to play with her nipples—rolling, pinching, and tugging. Her hips undulated as she moaned, enjoying her pleasure.

Moving the hand that had been stimulating her pebbled tips, she brought the vibrator to the entrance of her core and eased it inside. That's where she got it all wrong… she didn't need some small, vibrating toy slipping gently into her pussy. No, what she needed was a man's large, hard cock, throbbing as he steadied and mounted her, driving to the end of her sheath in one brutal lunge. He could almost feel how she would clamp down on his shaft, her cunt trembling along his length.

Sage was moving the toy in and out as she rubbed her clit. A man who knew what he was doing would be able to thrust in such a way, he'd hit her clit with every surge forward. She closed her eyes, throwing her head back, panting as her muscles stiffened in anticipation of her impending orgasm, moving the vibrator in and out at an increased pace as her climax washed over her. Sage took a deep breath and relaxed. She needed more. She needed a man who could and would ride her hard and long... and often, making her come repeatedly before emptying himself into her as she writhed beneath him.

"Sometimes, Roark, I wish you were real," she sighed, placing the vibrator on the nightstand.

Sage woke the next morning completely and utterly refreshed. She had a breakfast this morning with readers, a panel discussion, then the actual signing. She looked in the closet and laughed. Gail had packed her outfits for today in a garment bag labeled "Breakfast and Panel," "Signing," and a last one marked "Drive Home." She must think Sage was the most incompetent, unfashionable person in the world. She wasn't that far off the mark. It wasn't that she didn't know, but for the most part, she just didn't care.

Since she'd started making good money, she had indulged her love of gorgeous lingerie and corsets—expensive, handmade corsets. There was a place in London, very exclusive, she would love to visit. The problem was they catered to Doms, even though the corsets, thongs and other fet wear were meant for submissives. She was neither submissive nor in a relationship with any kind of Dom. She wrote about alpha males and dominant men but had never experienced either. She had tried to get Derek to go to one of the kink clubs in D.C. or try something outside of pure vanilla sex, but he had been adamantly opposed. She wondered if he still had those objections given that his new fiancée, Gwen, was one of her most avid readers.

Breakfast was fun once everyone calmed down about the incident the night before. Sage had followed the hotel and Gail's lead and passed it off as just drunken teenagers out on a lark. She was sponsoring the breakfast, so she had arranged small gift bags of swag to be at the place setting of each of those attending. Sage tried to include things that people would find useful—eyeglass wipes, pens, coasters, can koozies, and the like. She had also overridden Gail's plan for an enhanced continental breakfast, opting for a full buffet.

"I thought we agreed to go with the cheaper option," Gail hissed under her breath. "And where did all these swag bags come from?"

"I wanted something better for breakfast. I arranged for the swag bags weeks ago and had them delivered here. Lighten up, Gail… it's not like you're paying for it. This gets deducted after I calculate your percentage."

At the end of the breakfast, she stood and announced, "Everybody should have received a small gift at their place setting. At each table, I randomly placed a bag marked Winner. If you have the winning swag bag… stand up."

When each of the winners stood, Sage clapped her hands, and hotel staff brought in a gift basket for each of them. She was glad she'd reminded Gail this kind of thing didn't come out of her percentage… otherwise, Gail might have fetched them back.

"It looks like there is a forty-five-minute break until the panel starts in the room right across the hall," she announced.

"Sage? Will you be available for pictures between now and then?" called an attendee.

"Always! There's a beautiful little courtyard right outside these French doors. Anyone who wants to, let's go outside." She moved toward the exit. Seeing the size of the crowd, she added, "Anyone who doesn't get a picture now will have a chance after the panel or after the signing."

She smiled as she heard people calling their thanks. Sage tried to do everything she could to ensure her readers had a good time at events. She really didn't understand those who didn't. She understood that for some authors, these kinds of events were like pulling teeth, but others, in her opinion, had become too impressed with themselves to be bothered. Sage vowed never to be like them.

The combination of sunshine, fresh air, her readers' company and good cheer had completely banished the darkness from the night before. Sage entered the room for the panel discussion with her readers right before it was due to start and rushed up onto the raised dais.

Norma Sue Riley had been the queen of erotic romance before Sage had showed up on the scene and resented that Sage's sales made hers seem paltry in comparison.

"Finally decide to join us, Sage?" Norma Sue asked with more than a bit of venom in her tone. "I'm afraid the only seat left is the one on the end."

Sage and Norma Sue were not friends, and Sage was fairly sure Norma Sue had arranged for her to sit at the far end of the stage.

"That's alright, Norma Sue—some of us don't need to be center stage to let our light shine," she responded brightly.

Some of the other panelists tried to cover their laughter, while others, as well as those in the audience, didn't.

"This question is for Sage. Sage, who was your

inspiration for Roark, and as a follow-up, if he existed, would you fuck him?"

Sage laughed. "Follow-up first… absolutely and repeatedly." More laughter. "I guess Roark is a kind of amalgamation of a lot of the spies and detectives from movies of the past, but he's always been his own unique person. He just stepped forward one day and began telling me his story."

"Sage, how long did it take for your career to take off and how hard was it to write?" asked another audience member.

"I was incredibly lucky. My very first book hit big, thanks a lot to my publisher, Gail Vincent. You know, the first one wasn't so difficult, but the second one was a bitch. I was so afraid I would disappoint all of you."

"Sage, I have one for you," said Angelica Golden, a fellow author and friend. "What's the weirdest thing you've ever put in your butt?"

"Only the Queen of Butt Stuff would ask me that!" Sage said, laughing. "I don't know that I've done anything weird… just the normal stuff. Is that too much information?"

The questioning went on for the entire two hours scheduled, most of the questions coming to Sage, who tried her best to include some of the other authors. Most of them were easy and fun to answer until the final one…

The final question took her a bit by surprise.

"Sage, have you ever had a stalker, or has your fame ever caused you problems?"

"Not so far unless you count those of you that stalk me on Bookbub, Facebook, Instagram, and the like." Again, there was laughter. "I've been very lucky. I've known nothing but kindness and support from my readers, and I thank you all for that."

With that, the panel broke up. Her friend, Adaline Clark, leaned over and whispered, "I thought Norma Sue was going to have an apoplectic fit."

"Me, too. I can't decide whether or not I'm happy she didn't."

There was a two-hour break for lunch. Sage spent the time with readers, allowing them to take pictures with her, introducing them to Terrance, and encouraging them to take pictures with him as well. She would have forgotten lunch if one of her readers hadn't simply brought her some of the hotel's famous soup and decadent bread. Sage ensured both her lunch and that of the reader went on her tab. When the reader protested, Sage grinned and said, "Beat you to it."

Sage excused herself, running up to her room to freshen up and change. Entering her room on a high note, she smiled when she saw a beautiful bouquet waiting for her. There was a card attached, but she didn't take the time to open it. She stripped down and did a few yoga stretches before donning the outfit Gail had designated for the signing.

~

He watched as she stripped down to only her lacy bra and matching panties. While the bra was far more to his liking than those she had worn when he'd first seen her, the hip hugger panties still needed some work. She should wear a thong or better yet, nothing at all.

The next several hours were boring beyond measure. As usual, when he had the opportunity, he explored the boundaries of his prison and found no escape.

He heard her return, watching as she entered her room and walked to the table with the flowers in its center. Pulling the card out of the envelope, Sage shrieked and dropped it as if she had picked up a venomous snake. He watched as she backed away, never taking her eyes off the card,

scrambling backward toward the phone on the table by the bed. Picking it up, she asked for the manager.

"Ms. Matthews?"

"I think you should call the police and find out who delivered flowers to my room."

"Flowers? No one sent flowers to your room, Ms. Matthews."

Sage could never play poker. Her face was an open book and revealed all her emotions. She was confused, but confusion was quickly supplanted when a breeze ruffled her auburn locks and she looked up. He followed her gaze as best he could, but couldn't see what she saw.

"Now… come now! The door to the terrace…"

Her sentence was cut off by the bang on the door and two of the security team coming through it.

He pounded against the barrier between him, but he couldn't get to her.

"Ms. Matthews?" one of the guards said as the other opened the door.

"The flowers," she said, pointing. "How did they get here? Who brought them? The note?"

God, why couldn't he get to her! Damn it!

The manager of the hotel entered. "Ms. Matthews?"

"The note," she whispered.

The manager picked it up and read it, pale as he handed it to the security guard, who took it by the corner. "It says, 'Purveyors of Smut Must Die!'"

"We're going to call the police, Ms. Mathews," the manager said.

"No," Sage said a bit unsteadily.

No? What the fuck did she mean by no? They needed to get the police and make them understand Sage was in danger. That Sage didn't want to understand or accept she was in danger wasn't all that surprising. Her publisher had been right—she needed a keeper.

"But this is the second threat..." the head of security said.

"I know, but the signing starts," she said, glancing at her watch, "in a few minutes. I'm going to be in a crowded room here in the hotel, so I'll be safe. Honestly, I really can't let my readers down. Some of them have been planning for a year to be here."

The manager smiled. "All the staff keeps saying how nice you are, and that you're kind to your fans."

"Readers. They aren't my fans. They're my readers."

"I'll send three of my men down—one on each entrance and one circulating. We'll keep an eye on you. The police should be here any time. They'll want to look for forensic evidence here in your room and will probably take a look at where someone took a shot at you last night. I think we can all agree that Ms. Matthews was the target last night."

"Thank you so much. I really have to go. Can you take care of letting the police in and tell them I'll be happy to talk to them afterward?"

"Of course we can," the manager said, and allowed the security detail to take her to the ballroom for the signing.

"You don't think this is some kind of damn publicity stunt, do you?" the head of security asked after she'd left the room.

How dare they think that about Sage? She would never do anything like that, and if that idiot doesn't know that after talking to her and seeing the fear in her eyes, he isn't up to the job.

"I don't think so. Like I said, the staff all rave about how nice she is and that she's a really good tipper without being showy about it."

∽

Sage, a bit rattled, was escorted down to the signing. *Who would want to hurt her?* The idea someone did was a bit unnerving, but she had a job to do—one of the best parts of her job. She straightened her shoulders, tossed her hair back, and entered the signing room.

Seeing her table made her smile. Gail had come down earlier to set it up so Sage would have time to change. Her new stand-up sign made her smile, and the table was well organized, showing her books to their best advantage. There was room behind her and underneath for additional books and swag, giving her space to sign books and talk to readers—both new and old.

The next several hours sped by. Sage was engrossed with readers, selling and signing books, and participating in various giveaways. Gail fluttered around, spending most of her time with Sage but also talking with other authors she wanted to bring over to her publishing house.

"I have a small group of newbie authors I thought we could have a drink with. They'd love to talk with you, and one or two of them I'd like to land as clients," Gail whispered.

"Then why don't you…"

"Sage, sweetie, they don't want to talk to me. They want to talk to you. I could use your help."

Sage noticed Gail rarely asked, usually told, and never said please, but Gail had been the one to take a chance on her, and they had taken the niche publishing world by storm.

"Okay, but I promised the hotel manager I'd talk to the police before I left."

"The police? About last night?"

"Partially. Someone managed to get flowers and a somewhat threatening note into my suite."

"Oh my God, Sage." Gail squeezed her arm comfortingly. "Why didn't you say something?"

"Nothing happened, other than I was a bit spooked, but the police want to talk to me in light of what happened last night. Let me just make sure they aren't here. Why don't you start, and I'll join you as soon as possible?"

"I'll get them started, then join you. I don't want you to have to go through this alone."

"I'll be fine…"

"No, I want to be there for you."

For all her nagging and bossiness, Gail was a good friend and had been there every step of the way. Granted, her business had grown alongside Sage's, but she often went over and above what Sage felt most publishers would do.

As they left the ballroom, Gail headed toward the bar while Sage was met by the hotel manager.

"Ms. Matthews, the police are in your room and wondered if that would be a convenient place for you to speak to them?"

"That's fine."

They entered her room as a group of people, in what looked to be hazmat suits, exited.

"Ms. Matthews, I'm Detective Miller," a man said, walking forward and extending his hand.

Sage was always surprised when she met real-life detectives, who only occasionally resembled the tall, good-looking men who portrayed them in film and on television. Detective Miller was short, round, and balding. His skin was pale and slack, and she thought he looked as though he was more interested in retirement than what had happened to her.

"Detective Miller, please call me Sage." She looked back toward the door as the last technician left her room. "Should I be more worried than I am already?"

"Why? Oh, the protective gear? That's their standard garb to keep from contaminating evidence, not because we think there are hazardous materials."

"Good, I was a bit worried. I'm not sure what I can tell you, Detective, but I'm happy to cooperate."

"Why don't you tell me what happened?"

"Just today, or do you want me to start with last night?"

She wondered why he didn't seem to be up-to-speed on all that had happened. Didn't he see everything was connected… or at least it seemed to be?

"Do you think the two incidents are linked to one another?" the detective asked as he looked out the window.

"Don't you?" Sage asked incredulously. "I'm sorry, Detective, but am I boring you?"

"No, ma'am, but the report I had said everyone agreed it was just kids who got out of hand…"

"Because that's the way it appeared at the time," she said, stressing the last three words, "but given that I've now received a threatening note, I would think the idea of rowdy teenagers would be in question."

Sage was trying to quell her rising anger, but the idea that what had happened were separate, isolated incidents was absurd. She wasn't a trained investigator, but even she could see that.

"The two aren't necessarily connected," the detective said defensively.

Sage stared at him. "I think you're wrong, Detective. What's more, I think you know it. I think you know you fucked up last night and are more concerned about saving face than ensuring nothing else happens."

"I don't appreciate you speaking to me that way…"

"And I don't appreciate your cavalier attitude. Not to worry, though, Detective, I'm headed home today, so you can wash your hands of me."

Gail breezed in as Sage and the detective squared off. "Problem?"

Sage shook her head and drew herself up. "None at all. The detective is leaving. I was going to ask the manager if he could have my things packed and taken down to my car. I'll grab my computer, go down and meet with your authors, and leave immediately afterward."

Sage turned to leave, but Gail restrained her.

"Detective, as I'm sure you can imagine, Sage has been upset by what happened… artistic temperament. I'm sure you understand. Sage, the detective is just trying to do his job."

Artistic temperament? Since when did she have an artistic temperament? The idea that somehow she was blowing all of this out of proportion was absurd and was beginning to be annoying. Could it be that the detective was one of those people who thought that what she did for a living was wrong and that books like hers should be banned?

"No, the detective is pissed he got sent out here. Why is that Detective Miller? Do you not like what I write for a living?" Sage asked.

"You write smut, Ms. Matthews, and no, I don't like what you write. I think you give women all kinds of wrong ideas about what they should expect and want. I could get past that, but what I can't get past is the idea that both of these attempts, and I put that in air quotes, never even came close to hurting you, and you artistic types are fond of publicity stunts."

Sage turned to him. "You think I staged this?"

The detective nodded. "I do. The shots weren't all that close, and there is absolutely no evidence anyone broke in here…"

∽

But there was. He'd heard someone enter when Sage was out of her room. He hadn't been able to see who it was, but he was certain it wasn't Sage. She was in danger, and the idiot they'd assigned to her case didn't want to see it or was too dim to understand. He'd never resented the barrier between them more than he did at that moment.

∽

"And with that," Sage said melodramatically, "the artistic porn writer swept out of the room." She could hear Gail making apologies, then rushing down the hall to catch up with her.

"Really, Sage, that was not the best way to handle that."

"The man pretty much accused me of arranging what happened. He has zero interest in finding out who did this, much less why."

"You must admit, it would be good publicity…"

Sage stopped and looked at her.

"Gail, please tell me you didn't do this," she whispered.

"Of course not, I'm just saying it would be good publicity."

CHAPTER 3

Several Months Later

Sage stopped at the quaint post office in town. Each time she entered the small building, she smiled as Betty, the local postmistress, greeted her.

"Good morning, Sage. Lots of mail waiting for you. How's the new book coming?"

"Roark is being his usual self… but that's what my readers want."

Betty had been the postmistress for as long as anyone could remember. She reminded Sage of a small bird with her silver-white hair, colorful earrings, and bespectacled eyes that missed little to nothing. When Sage had first moved here, she'd been worried if the proper little lady, born and raised in the Bible belt, found out what kind of books she wrote, she'd be run out of town.

Contrary to her fears, Betty was a voracious reader and loved Sage's books. She'd become one of Sage's ARC readers and a part of her online focus group.

"We adore Roark. He's such a bad boy... but he's so good at being one. He always saves the damsel in distress and,"—she looked around to ensure no one else was there— "he gives them so many orgasms. I tell you, my dear, Wendell has upped his game since I started reading your books."

Sage laughed and opened her post office box, removing her mail. She stood by the trash can, tossing the junk mail, then placed all but one of the remaining pieces in the large tote she carried as her purse. She looked at the envelope and frowned—nothing really notable about it other than the fact it had no return address and a postmark from Hilton Head, South Carolina. She didn't know anyone in South Carolina, at least not anyone who'd have her post office box address.

"What's wrong, Sage?" Betty asked.

"I'm not sure. There's an envelope with no return address and postmarked from Hilton Head."

"Reader?"

"I wouldn't think so. Nobody but close friends know this address, and I don't know anyone from there."

"Still worried about what happened at the Huntington?"

"I don't know that I'm worried, but it's a bit

unsettling. I had my security system upgraded after I found the hole in the back fence. I'd feel better if someone took it seriously, but I'm pretty sure Detective Miller is convinced it's just a publicity stunt."

"Well, it didn't help when Ms. Vincent put the word out to the media. I've seen several of the interviews you did…"

"I know. I made Gail tie the interviews to new releases after the first one, but each time I do one, someone wants to know about the shooting and the flowers. I wish Gail had never said anything."

"Hey, Sage!" a deputy said.

Sage turned and looked at Betty. She wouldn't put it past the wizened postmistress to have alerted the local sheriff's office about the letter. With anyone else, she might have thought it was invasive, but she knew Betty cared about her and knew the incident at the signing and the break-in had spooked Sage.

"Charlie, it's nice to see you. Let me guess… it's not a surprise you're here."

"Betty did mention you got a suspicious letter. Why don't we take it over to the office and open it there? We can dust it for prints and look for other clues."

"So, you don't think it's a publicity stunt?" she asked hopefully.

"I don't know if it is or isn't,"—he held up his hand to stave off her argument— "but I know if it is, you aren't behind it. I wouldn't put it past that pushy New York publisher of yours."

"You know, just because she isn't from the South doesn't make her the bad guy."

"She's not from around here, so I don't trust her."

"Charlie, I'm not a local…" she started.

"You are now," Betty asserted.

"Yes, ma'am." Charlie grinned. "You may not have been born in these parts, but you've become a part of the community. There's not anyone in town who doesn't think of you as one of us."

Sage smiled. "Thanks, Charlie. That means a lot to me."

Charlie escorted her back to the office and carefully opened the envelope after dusting it for prints.

"I don't think we'll find anything."

"There seem to be lots of prints," Sage said.

"Yes, but I suspect they're postal employees. Luckily, they're all fingerprinted, so we can eliminate them. I'm just hoping whoever he is got sloppy."

"Why do you think it's a guy?"

"Two-thirds of the women stalked are stalked by a past intimate partner, most of them male."

"That should narrow the pool. Not a lot of guys in my past." *At least not a lot who know who I am.*

Charlie finished his examination, and they went to lunch. He was sweet, charming, and a little shy.

Sage thought he was NGB—Nice Guy But—absolutely nothing wrong with him, a perfectly lovely guy, yet she couldn't imagine getting involved with him. She might be wrong, but she was fairly certain if he was anything other than straight vanilla, it was only vanilla with a few birthday sprinkles.

Sage had found to truly experience and revel in sex, she needed more. Not pain for pain's sake, but dominance, so she could shed her own need for control, relax, and just enjoy. She often wondered if Gail might benefit from the same. Sage had found it was better to frequent high-end kink clubs where everything was negotiated beforehand and confidentiality was assured.

Sage was certain no one from any of the clubs would be stalking her. She felt safer in most of the clubs than she did anywhere else.

∽

The new Roark Samuels book wasn't coming along as well as the ones that had come before. The fact was she had an alpha wolf shifter who kept growling at her to tell his story, and she was trying to ignore him in order to finish Roark's new novel. Sometimes, when she found a sex scene wasn't coming along the way she wanted, she'd slip into a sexy corset and thong to write. If that didn't work, she'd turn up the music and take a break, singing and dancing in her solarium. She couldn't dance and was an awful singer, but she enjoyed it, and sometimes, the break from the grind and the endorphins from moving around freed up her creativity.

Gail liked to tease her about her penchant for dressing up when there was nobody home, confessing she often stayed in her pajamas if she didn't go into her office. Sage figured she was the only one there, so it didn't matter if others thought her weird. There was something about singing and dancing around the large space, especially at night under the stars, which helped her think.

～

He watched her dance. He loved when she danced in the solarium—a private show just for him. Once or twice, she'd forsaken the lingerie and danced naked. He watched as she swung her body around and moved gracefully across the floor. He couldn't understand why she didn't think she could dance. He'd heard her say to herself and others that she moved like an ungainly foal on a set of roller skates. But she was wrong. She had an innate beauty, style, and sense of rhythm that made her an excellent dancer. Like many things, Sage's shortcomings were all in her head. He'd love to take her dancing—someplace dark with soft, sultry music, so he could press her body against his. He longed to have her in his embrace, her arms wrapped around his neck, hip-to-hip as his hands cupped her ass, holding her close, but more than that, he wanted her naked and in his bed.

Even thinking of Sage naked was enough to make his recalcitrant cock aching and hard. She was so fucking hot and so completely ignorant of that fact. The idiot she had once been engaged to was a fool. A woman like Sage was a rare and marvelous creature to be cherished. He knew she hadn't had sex with a man in a while, and he was much larger than her vibrator. He wanted to lay her down, spread her legs, and make a place for himself there, shoving his cock balls deep up inside her.

Watching her, he wrapped his hand around his shaft and began to stroke, sweeping his hand from its weeping head all the way back to its root. He needed to maintain control. He'd managed to manipulate the phone system in a way that when her fence was breached, he had the security company come out and convince her she needed to upgrade her system.

God, how he'd wanted to put her over his knee and spank her gorgeous ass when she'd refused to call the cops. Granted, the police at the signing event had been less than helpful, but she had to know the deputy sheriff with the puppy-dog eyes here in her hometown would have believed her. Neither Sage nor the deputy had figured out how he found out about the breach. The deputy might be attractive, but he was dumb as a rock and not at all what Sage wanted—he wasn't always sure Sage knew what she wanted.

Now she'd received a letter. It had unsettled her, and thankfully, the deputy had followed her back to the house after she received it. She'd scanned and sent it to Gail, so he knew what it said. *"You have been warned. Your filth must be stopped!"* Her note to Gail had said there had been no return address, but the postmark showed it had been sent from Hilton Head. Sage didn't know anyone who lived there.

She tried to hit a high note and missed. He groaned, only partly in response to the sensations his cock continued to experience from his ministrations. Sage could be taught to be a wonderful dance partner, but she would never be able to sing. There were a number of things he wanted to teach her—how to shiver from his whisper of her name along her skin, how to climax just from his mounting her, and how to call him Sir or Master when she came.

He increased the speed of his stroke, closing his eyes and imagining how much better it would feel if it was Sage's pussy spasming all up and down his length. He would spread her thighs, hooking them in his elbows so she had nowhere to hide. She would learn she belonged to him, and he would look and play with whatever he liked, whenever he liked, and as often as he liked. He would make her take everything he had to give her, holding nothing back, and screaming her need for him when he'd forced numerous climaxes from her body as he filled her pussy to overflowing.

As his imagination ran rampant, his body stiffened, and his warm, creamy seed spilled out, covering his fist. He pumped until he'd emptied himself. When he was finally done, his muscles relaxed, and his breathing returned to normal. He had to find a way to get to her. They would be so good together.

∽

"Let's see, Roark, what should I have you do to this one? The readers love it when they sass you, and you feed them your cock after spanking them, then fuck them from behind. I don't think you've taken one of their asses that way in a while. Now, what should she do, and where should she do it…"

Sage cackled. As usual, her physical release, singing, and dancing had helped immensely. The words started to flow. She loved when the writing came so easily, she could barely type fast enough to keep up with the words as they came into her head, describing the scene. Sage turned up the music and typed, absorbed in the work, and the hours sped by. By the time she looked up, dawn was beginning to creep over the horizon.

She hit save and stood, stretching her arms overhead and arching side to side. She kissed her fingertips and pressed them to her favorite Roark Samuels' cover she'd had made into a piece of stretched canvas art.

"I'll see you later, Roark," she said, and headed up to her bedroom to take a shower.

~

When Sage's cell phone rang, she glanced at the caller ID and sighed. It was Gail. Sage knew if she ignored her, Gail would just call back.

"Well?" Gail said without preliminaries.

"I'm almost done. Just wrote the last sex scene. I need to do a wrap up where he hands the heiress off to her wimpy fiancé, and she longingly watches him walk off into the sunset. It should be done before the end of the day." Taking a deep breath, she continued. "This is the last Roark Samuels novel… at least for a while. I thought I'd take a little vacation and start a new paranormal series."

"You live at the beach. How much more vacation do you need? As for that silly werewolf idea…"

"Not werewolves, wolf-shifters," she said, enthusiastic about sharing her idea. "There's no tortured transition into some grotesque, misbegotten shape, just one minute you're human, then a kind of shimmer, then you're a wolf…"

"Whatever. Roark Samuels sells. You can do a vanity project next year."

"It's not a vanity project, Gail. I need to grow as an author, to hone my craft—"

"For Christ's sake, Sage, Roark pays the bills."

"The books are predictable. Sometimes, it feels like all that changes are the names and the locales… well, more than that. I mean, I work really hard to keep things fresh and always keep them guessing about what's going to happen, but they are becoming a bit formulaic."

"People like predictable. They know what to expect from you. It can't be that taxing. Hell, Sage, anyone could write them. It's not like you're ever going to be the next Nora Roberts. You simply don't have that kind of talent, but few do."

"Then I guess it's a good thing I don't want to be Nora Roberts or any other romance writer. I like being me and fortunately for both of us, so do my readers."

They had this argument each time Sage neared the completion of a novel. In the end, she always capitulated and did what Gail wanted—without Gail, she would never have had a career, something Gail always reminded her of—but the other characters in her head were vying for her attention. She'd even started a wolf-shifter and a bear-shifter, but both times, Roark had asserted himself and intrigued her with a new twist on his normal plot lines.

"Look, sweetie," Gail continued. "I know I've been a tough taskmaster of late, but I have to work hard on your behalf, and you don't want to let your fans down. They'd be so disappointed if you retired Roark. And what would everyone say if your next novel failed? You don't want them to say you're just a one-trick pony—that if it isn't Roark that you can't write it."

"But that's what worries me. What if I am?"

"You won't know that for sure unless you write something new and different, and it falls flat on its face. I know you've read the articles about picking your lane and staying in it. It's the best way to expand your market. I've worked so hard to put you and Roark on the map and everyone's Kindle."

"But maybe my readers would like it if we took a different road, a path less traveled."

"Sage, sweetie, less traveled means less money."

"I make enough money…" Sage started.

"There is no such thing as enough money. Come on, you can do a couple more before the end of the year, don't you think? I'll tell you what, why don't you finish the next two, then you and I will sneak away for a long weekend in London. We'll eat at all the best restaurants, shop in the best stores, see a play in the West End… maybe even see if we can get you into that club… what's it called?"

"You know perfectly well it's Baker Street, and you know how much I'd like to go there." Sage knew she was being played. "Let me guess, we'd go about the same time as the London book signing?"

Gail laughed. It occurred to Sage her laugh never sounded as though it was filled with joy or even much amusement.

"It would allow you to write off all the expenses of our trip," Gail said. "Come on, we'll have fun, and I'll make all the arrangements."

Sage rolled her eyes, glad they weren't on a video call. She was well aware what Gail meant was that she'd book them first-class tickets on the plane, arrange for them to stay in the best hotel, and allow Sage to pick up the entire cost of the trip. She also knew it was pointless to argue with Gail. For one thing, they *would* have a good time, and for the other, Gail could be relentless when she wanted something. While her public might think of Sage as tough, dominant, and in charge of her own life, Gail knew different and knew just which buttons to push and how to get what she wanted.

"I guess that would be nice. Could we stay at the Savoy?"

"The event is at the Four Seasons. It would be more convenient to be there, and I prefer it."

Again, she rolled her eyes, then she had an idea that would allow her to stay at the Savoy and would appeal to Gail's penchant for drama.

"What if you stay at the Four Seasons, and I stay at the Savoy? We can rent a Rolls Royce limo and driver while we're there. You could set it up so I make a grand entrance, and you could control access to me. Besides, Roark lives at the Savoy. It would strengthen my brand. They've always said they'd give me a discount…"

"Hmm… and maybe we could have a small gathering there for industry people. Not a bad idea, Sage. Leave it all to me. And don't bother packing anything except the outfits I bought you for the signing at the Huntington. The last time I visited, I went through your closet. We're going to need to go through it and purge a lot of your things. I can get a few things here for you in New York. If we go early enough, I can pick you up some more suitable things in London. They really do have some of the most amazing shops. I know a lot of people rave about Paris, but they're so Parisian. I much prefer London. I'll get something for you to wear over and bring it down. You can drive in from your little island and spend the night, then we can fly out of Charlotte."

"Don't you think we should shop together? I think I may have put on a little weight."

"Yes, I noticed. Not to worry. A good set of Spanx, the right tailor, and you'll look perfect. I'll see if Henri can't come down to do your hair. Don't do anything to it until he gets there. Agreed? Of course you do. You're such a dear girl and my favorite author."

Before Sage could get in another word, the line was dead.

Oh well, at least I get to stay at the Savoy, and maybe if I tip the driver enough, I can see a bit of London.

She picked up the paperback of her latest novel and smiled. Roark wasn't the hunk du jour—he wasn't blond, pretty, and polite. He was tall, dark, and lethal, with a strong, muscular physique. He had black hair, chocolate eyes, chiseled features, and the requisite six-pack abs—actually an eight-pack—and a pronounced V-formation that led to his sizeable cock, which rarely seemed to tire. Roark was arrogant, demanding, quick to spank, and even quicker to fuck, and like her readers, she was just a little bit in love with him.

She sighed. Too bad guys like him didn't exist outside romance novels.

The phone rang.

"Hello?"

There was nothing but silence on the other end—silence and heavy breathing. Sage glanced at the phone, which showed 'Unknown' on the caller ID.

"Who is this?" she asked, keeping her voice steady.

"You can't get people all hot and bothered, then not put out," said a quiet, raspy voice.

Sage tried to keep from panicking. How the hell

had he gotten her cell phone number? She was assuming based on what Charlie had said it was a man, since there really wasn't any way to tell for certain.

"Why are you doing this to me? What have I ever done to you?"

"You're breathing, aren't you?" the voice said, cackling as the line went dead.

She tried to remember what buttons you were supposed to push to get some kind of caller ID but couldn't. She called the Sheriff's Office and reported the call to Charlie, who told her not to call anyone else and he was on his way.

Within minutes, Sage could hear sirens, and for once, was glad someone was making a fuss. The call had been unnerving. She checked the alarm system, and everything showed as working properly, but still, she shivered with fear.

She glanced at the Roark Samuels cover hanging on the wall, then down at her laptop.

"I really wish you were here, Roark. I'm beginning to think I could use a hero right about now."

When she heard the patrol vehicle pull up, she walked out to let Charlie in.

∾

He tried to see if he could figure out where the call that had so unsettled her had come from. Who the fuck was stalking her, and why wasn't Deputy Puppy Eyes doing more about it? He pounded on the barrier and tried to see if he could hear and see more of what was going on. He couldn't, but was grateful when he heard footsteps coming back into the solarium.

"Sage, you shouldn't have opened the door without confirming it was me," the lawman admonished.

"Who else has the security code to the front gate? I could see it was your SUV, so don't treat me like a child."

Therein lay the problem. She wasn't a child, but she desperately needed boundaries, rules, and consequences for breaking them. His cock began to swell when he thought of all the consequences he'd like to impose on Sage for her naughty behavior, beginning with a discipline spanking that would leave her rounded globes red and stinging, her nipples pebbled, and her pussy wet and ripe for the taking.

He snorted. That boy in the deputy's uniform didn't have a clue what it would take to dominate a woman like Sage—make her feel loved and safe enough she could embrace her submissive side. Even if he could recognize it, the boy didn't have what it took to give her what she needed and desired in the deepest part of her soul.

If he could just break through the veil that separated them and figure out a way to stay with her, he could give her everything she needed. Sometimes when she slept, he was able to reach through and be with her, if only for a few hours. While it was real and tactile for him, Sage, if she remembered it at all, did so as a dream. She always woke the next day relaxed, refreshed, and focused on whatever she needed to do. It was as if when she needed him most and allowed her self-protective walls to crumble just a bit, her soul reached out to his and he was able to break through.

"No need to get feisty on me. I'm here to help, remember?" the deputy scolded.

Feisty? The idiot didn't understand her at all. She wasn't feisty. She was fierce, tough, strong, and beautiful, longing for a partner she could lean on— one who wouldn't take advantage of her but provide her with the stability and structure that would allow her to flourish and do so happily.

"I'm sorry, Charlie," Sage sighed. "Of course, you're right… at least about the part that I know you're trying to help. It was just a bit unnerving."

"I understand," he said, taking her hand. "With your permission, I'm going to have your calls traced, but I doubt we'll get anything."

"Where are my manners? Can I get you something to drink?"

"No, I'm good. I called your alarm company, and they're running a full system check. If you'd like, I'll go through the house, then walk the property. Before I leave, I'll make sure the security folks give the system the a-okay and will make sure you're all tucked in."

If the idiot was a real man and had half a clue, he'd make sure he was tucked in next to her, providing her with everything she needed. Well, fuck the security company and her cell phone provider. He'd figured out how to check in with those systems. He couldn't actually jump into them, but he could communicate with them and get information.

CHAPTER 4

End of October

It had been two months since she had received the phone call. Charlie had shared with her that they had traced the call to a burner phone —one that had been discovered at the Cape Hatteras lighthouse, so whoever he was, he'd been close. Sage had arranged for the number he'd called to be sent to a recorder, then had the one for her phone changed. So far, so good. She hadn't had any calls. Gail had come down the week before, new clothes, tailor, and hairstylist in tow.

It was a clear, crisp, October day on the North Carolina coast when she pulled the vintage roadster out of the garage and headed down the long drive. Sage knew both the roadster and the house were huge indulgences, but she loved them both. She often thought she could live in a smaller house as long as she could have an office like her solarium and live on the beach, but she adored her car. She also had an SUV for bad weather and if she needed to take more than just her and her luggage. The antique sports car wasn't practical, but it was beautiful and luxurious… and she loved to drive it.

Sage had knocked her automatic gate opener off of the seat next to her. Normally, she kept it on the visor, but when she was going to hit the highway at speed, she always worried about it somehow flying off, so she would remove it and place it on the passenger seat of the car. She was slowing down and making the turn as she leaned down to get it. When she sat back up, she slammed on the brakes, even though she had plenty of room, and managed to stifle the small scream that threatened to escape.

There, hanging from the arch over the gate, was a dangling body—a figure obviously meant to be her—and sticking out of its chest was a large knife. She glanced up as she drove underneath and was pretty sure that it was a real body and not just a mannequin or dummy of some sort. Sage shivered. It was frightening to know someone had done that… and that they knew where she lived.

She dialed the Sheriff's Office.

Sheriff Larsen answered.

"Sheriff, it's Sage Matthews."

"How can we help, Ms. Matthews? We haven't heard anything else on your case…"

"Well, you might want to come out to the house. Someone left an effigy of me with a knife through the heart, hanging from the archway over my gate."

"What the hell?" She could hear him scrambling and calling to their dispatcher. "Are you all right?"

"I am, but I'm on my way to Charlotte. I need to meet with some people this evening, then I'm taking an overnight flight to London. I'll be there at least a week. Can I just leave this and close the gate behind me?"

"Yes, ma'am, if that's what you need to do, but I don't want you to stop on your trip into Charlotte, and let us know you got there safely, okay? But my advice, and preference, would be that you not go at all."

"I can appreciate that, Sheriff, but this is part and parcel of my job, and I won't be intimidated. I hate to feel like I'm dumping this on you, but I'm a bit freaked out. It feels like whatever it is, it's escalating."

"I agree. Do me a favor, leave your car with the valet parking at the airport? I'll have Charlie fetch it back here. If you let us know when you're coming in, we'll meet you. I'd rather you didn't leave it unattended."

"Thanks, Sheriff, I really appreciate it. I hate to be such a bother."

"Not a bother at all, Ms. Matthews. I don't like

the idea that some looney is harassing one of my citizens."

Sage smiled. Small town Carolina life was very different from D.C.

The sky was a bright blue with large, white, fluffy clouds stirring around. The color of the sky was what she always thought of as Carolina Blue, and it seemed somehow clearer than other skies or even those closer to Charlotte. As she approached the main highway, she pulled on her Sage Matthews sequined ball cap and picked up speed. She roared down the highway, her state-of-the-art and most definitely 'not original equipment' stereo blaring away so she could sing at the top of her lungs. She wasn't a particularly good singer, but she didn't care; she loved to sing and in the car, speeding down the road, she could offend no one.

The six-hour trip in the fresh air cleared her head and allowed her to banish the vestiges of fear that had threatened to settle on her when she'd left earlier in the day. She pulled up to the hotel and was greeted by the concierge, who had both a bellboy and a parking valet with him. They'd rented a room so that they had a place to take a break and get ready for the overnight flight to London. The flight left at a little after midnight and would arrive sometime around noon.

"Ms. Matthews, how nice to see you again. Ms. Vincent called and should be here any time. We sent the car to the airport for her. She called and asked that you wait for her to have dinner. Sheriff Larsen called and told us of that nasty business at the end of your drive earlier today. That must have given you a fright… especially this time of year. With your permission, we've made a slight change in plans. We're going to put your car in a secure area, and his deputy will be in to pick it up tomorrow. We'll have the hotel's executive town car take you to the airport, and we've arranged with the airline for VIP check-in for both you and Ms. Vincent. If it's all right with you, might I suggest we have room service deliver your meal tonight and maybe something before you leave?"

"I hate for you to have to go to all this trouble…"

"Oh, it's no trouble at all. I guess this is the downside of being a celebrity."

Sage laughed. "I'm a far cry from being a celebrity, but thank you."

They unloaded her things, and she was escorted upstairs by the bellboy and two men from hotel security. When they entered the room, one of the guards stayed with her while the other swept the two-bedroom suite she and Gail would share.

"Don't get me wrong, I really appreciate this, but don't you think this is a bit much?"

The man shook his head. "No, ma'am. Sheriff Larsen called and talked to the hotel manager and my boss. He was pretty clear; they feel whoever left that figure hanging in front of your drive isn't just trying to spook you. The boss was just finalizing a few things but will be up to speak with you in just a few minutes."

Sage paled and nodded. The sheriff must have been spooked to have gone to this kind of trouble. When given the all-clear, she entered her room, tipped the bellman, and closed the door behind them. She was looking out the floor to ceiling window at the beautiful view of the city when she heard the key card in the lock. She startled and realized she was more keyed up than she thought. She smiled when Gail entered with a man she assumed was the head of security.

"Ms. Matthews, I'm Daryl Gutherie. I'm the head of security here at the hotel. Ms. Vincent is staying with you?"

"Sage, what the hell is going on?" Gail said, clearly outraged.

"Yes, Mr. Gutherie. Gail is with me." Turning to Gail, she said, "There's been another incident at the house."

"Oh my God, Sage! Are you all right?"

"Yes, but I left without knowing much… oh shit, I need to call Sheriff Larsen…"

"Not to worry, Ms. Matthews, I've taken care of that," the security guard said. "We advise you to have dinner and stay here in your room. I'm going to leave a man stationed outside your door. When you're ready, let him know, and he'll arrange to bring the food in and get you outside to the town car in the morning."

"The thing hanging from the archway..." said Sage to the deputy.

"Was a real body..." The head of security reached out to steady her. "He called the local doctor who doubles as a medical examiner. The body was hung after it was dead. They believe the corpse was stolen from a local funeral home."

Gail and Sage exchanged glances.

"Does that mean something to you two ladies?"

"Yes, I have a book that features, for lack of a better term, a stalker who does the same thing."

"Forgive me, I'm not familiar with your work, but can you tell me the title?" he asked.

"The Well-Hung Corpse," Sage said.

"Is it well known?"

Sage nodded. "Yes, it made the USA Today Bestseller list."

"It landed in the Top 10. I know your gift shop carries all of Sage's books in paperback..."

"If you like, I can send you a copy of the e-book. It might be easier for you to search for things electronically than doing it by hand," Sage offered.

"Thank you, ma'am, that would help. Now, don't worry. You're safe here with us, and we've alerted the airline and airport security in London.

I'll let you ladies settle in. If you need anything, you call down to the front desk. Don't open the door unless it's me or one of the two men you've already met."

"Okay, thank you, Mr. Gutherie."

The evening went smoothly, and both she and Gail were able to relax and get ready for the trip. Sage offered to sign the copies of her books the hotel had on hand and did so before they left. Their stay was quiet and uneventful.

They were ushered into a VIP Lounge in the airport, then given special boarding passes for first-class.

Gail whispered, "This is kind of nice... we should be treated like this all the time."

Sage smiled. "I don't know, Gail. It just seems a bit much."

They were escorted to their seats at the front of the plane. Sage was glad Gail had insisted. It was a long flight to London and flying in the upgraded seats made all the difference. Airport security met them on the plane and helped them deboard ahead of the rest of the passengers, remaining with her and Gail and personally conducting them through customs at Heathrow.

Word of her arrival, and the latest activity by her stalker, had been leaked to the press, who in turn, informed the public. Just beyond the secure area of the airport, both reporters and readers waited. Sage suspected the leak had been Gail's well-oiled publicity machine. Right before they had gone into a holding pattern over the airport in preparation to land, Gail had insisted she touch up her makeup and ensure her hair looked picture-perfect—literally. Tired as she was, complying was easier than not.

As they approached Customs, Gail poked Sage between the shoulder blades.

"Shit, Gail. That hurts."

"Don't slouch," Gail hissed.

"I'm tired. I didn't get any sleep on the plane."

"I know… and it shows, but the press and your fans…"

"I wish you wouldn't call them that."

"But that's what they are," Gail insisted.

Sage turned and stopped Gail's forward progression.

"No. They are my readers. If they're 'fans,' that puts me on a stupid pedestal. We have a symbiotic relationship. Without me, they don't have books to read they enjoy, but without them, I don't have a business. I know you don't think it's an important distinction, but I do."

Gail snorted. "Don't get your feathers ruffled. I forget part of your brand is your approachability."

Sage barely controlled rolling her eyes. It wasn't a part of any brand. It was who she was and how she felt. She and Gail often argued at book signings.

Gail didn't think Sage should sign a book for anyone or give them swag unless they bought a book. Sage just ignored her. If someone came by the table and talked to her, she gave them swag. If they brought a book or anything else and wanted her to sign it, she did. It was that simple and one of the things she stood firm on.

In some things—a lot of things, if she was honest—Gail was right. Her readers had come out to see her, and they deserved to see her looking her best. Sage straightened her spine, pasted on a bright smile, and made it through British Airport security and the reporters, who only shouted questions about the stalker. One of the security personnel, a short, slight girl with curly strawberry red hair, pulled her aside.

"I'm a big fan, Ms. Matthews. The airline has a small conference room right over here. Would you like to commandeer it for your fans?"

Sage's smile of relief was genuine. She couldn't think of anything that would revive her more.

"Readers," she corrected automatically. "I don't call the people who read my books fans. It sets up a power differential I'm not comfortable with. And yes, that would be wonderful." She turned to Gail. "Could you see if you can find someone to bring refreshments…"

"Sage," Gail started, "if you're going to spend some time, it should be with the reporters."

"The reporters get paid to come out here and see if they can get a story. My readers came to see me. If any reporters want to stick around and don't bother my readers, I'll talk to them."

The security officer escorted her and her readers to the conference room, where she was met by a representative of the airline.

"Maggie said you'd make time to sign books and talk to your fans. I've never read your stuff before, but I will now. I think it's so nice of you to get off a plane and make time for your fans," the airline official said.

Sage spent the next two hours with her readers. Nothing else could have refreshed her spirit the way they did—nothing. Perhaps if she'd had a man she could truly share her life with, but she'd decided when her engagement broke up, it was probably best just to go it alone.

After the last book had been signed, Sage remained where she was and allowed Gail to usher in a group of reporters and spent the next three hours answering questions. When it was over, Sage was relieved to learn Gail had indeed hired a Rolls Royce limo and driver for the duration of their trip. Sage insisted they drop Gail and everything they would need for the signing at the Four Seasons first before proceeding to the Savoy.

"I've called the Savoy and given them your wake-up calls, as well as the times the driver will be there to pick you up. I've also given the driver the schedule and arranged for you to have dinner tonight and breakfast tomorrow in your room." Gail admonished her before she got out of the limo.

"Isn't breakfast included in the signing event?" Sage asked.

"Yes, dear, but you don't want to be caught with food in your mouth if someone asks you a question." Gail gave her two air kisses, then got out after her luggage, all the books, and other event paraphernalia had been unloaded. The driver got back into the limo.

"Next stop… the Savoy."

"Would you mind terribly just driving me around a little so I can see something of the city?"

"Ms. Vincent was quite clear in her instructions."

"What Ms. Vincent doesn't know won't kill her, and I've got fifty pounds sterling that says you can keep a secret."

The driver grinned. "I can indeed."

The man had grown up in London, so he easily navigated not only the most popular routes, but those that had picturesque mews, cobblestone streets, and quaint shops. He dropped her at the Savoy, ensured her bags were taken up to her room, then the concierge accompanied her to the front desk, promising a smooth check-in.

"Will there be anything else, Ms. Matthews?"

the concierge asked while the bellman unpacked the last of her things. "We're all enormous fans and think it's wonderful you have Roark Samuels living here at the Savoy."

"I've always thought this was the best hotel in the world and was thrilled when your marketing manager gave me permission," Sage replied, smiling and handing him a large tip.

"Well, why wouldn't she? You're kind of a big deal."

"No, I'm not. Back then, I was nobody, and I do write pretty steamy stuff. I was just writing my first novel, but she was always so helpful. I could email her questions about hotel details and she'd give them to me. It allowed me to lend a sense of realism to the books." When the bellman finished unloading her luggage, Sage tipped him and thanked both him and the concierge for all their help.

"Very good, Miss. Your evening meal has been arranged, and I can either have it sent up immediately or give you time for a bath."

"What did Gail order for me?"

"A Caesar salad with grilled chicken, no croutons, and light dressing. Would you prefer something else?"

"What's good? What would you have?"

The concierge grinned. "Our shepherd's pie is second to none, then I'd add our truffled mash and the crushed mint peas, mixed together. Top it off with our vanilla crème brûlée."

"That sounds so much better."

"I will take care of it. And allow me to substitute the breakfast she ordered."

"Perfect," Sage said, smiling.

"Sweet or savory for breakfast?"

"A bit of both."

"Very well, Ms. Matthews. Would you like to take a bath before or after dinner?"

"A bath would be lovely."

"Shall I have it drawn for you?" he asked helpfully.

"No, thank you. I can manage. How about if you give me an hour?"

"Very good, Miss," he said before withdrawing.

Sage started the bathwater and smiled at the various fragrances she could add, opting for a light mix of vanilla and lavender. The combined aroma of the steam coming out of the tub was nothing short of divine.

Sage wandered back into her room while the water ran and carefully undressed, donning the Savoy-provided robe, and hung up her outfit. She had to admit Gail had exceptional taste—expensive, but exquisite. She returned to the bath and removed her makeup, wrapping her hair in a towel provided for just that use. Testing the water, she removed her robe and stepped into the tub, sighing as she slid down slowly so the water embraced her like a lover's caress. Who was she kidding? It had been so long since she'd experienced any sexual gratification that wasn't mutually negotiated at a club, she'd pretty much forgotten what true intimacy felt like.

After finishing her bath, she added moisturizer to her face and luxuriated in the Savoy's body lotion. Fluffing her hair, she pulled on a robe and allowed the room service waiter into the room to set her dinner up on the table. Sage had opened her laptop and had it sitting on the desk. She had decided if this trip was going to cost her an arm and a leg, she was going to enjoy it. The first bite of her dinner made her relax back in the chair and moan in pure delight. The concierge had been right, it was heaven, and the rest of her meal had been even better.

After dinner, she worked on the latest Roark Samuels novel but found she was having trouble getting into it. After a frustrating hour where she deleted scenes as soon as she'd written them, she gave up and got ready for bed. She walked over to look out the window onto the thriving metropolis. It was such a harmonious mix of old and new. Sage wondered briefly about all those who had inhabited the city—walked its streets, making lives for themselves, and about all of those who had used the great river for transportation and recreation. Smiling, she removed her robe, placed it on the edge of her bed, stretched, and got into bed. Sage's head had barely hit the pillow before she was fast asleep.

～

"That's it, sweetheart," he said softly. "Close your eyes and sleep."

He watched as the covers rose and fell with her breathing. When they'd first met, Sage had slept in a bra, tank top, and boy shorts. That pencil pusher who'd shared her bed hadn't been much on romance and had the stamina of a weakened old man on his death bed. One and done Derek, he called him. He'd barely play with Sage before rolling on top of her or letting her get on top. A couple of thrusts and Derek would come, pulling out and snoring shortly thereafter. Sage only managed to achieve a climax when she took charge and was on top or when she finished herself.

If and when, no… when, he admonished himself, when he managed to break out, she wouldn't be allowed to wear anything in bed. She would be available to him so he could pull her underneath him anytime he woke and wanted her. He would also forbid her from trying to pleasure herself. He would be in charge of all things sexual, and she would never be allowed on top. Sage had a bad habit, if given the slightest bit of rein, of taking the bit in her teeth and running. No, better to never allow her any sexual position, which in any way, shape, or form, allowed her to forget who was doing the fucking and who was being fucked.

He loved the way the bed covering outlined and emphasized her shape. Sage was not petite. She was tall with an hour-glass figure. She had hips a man could hold on to when he fucked her, and her ass was a thing of perfection. She was, quite simply, the sexiest woman he'd ever seen or that she'd ever created with her writing. He couldn't understand why all the women in her novels were skinny brats. No doubt that was the reason Roark didn't stay with them.

He pushed on the veil between them and felt it give way. She was exhausted, which meant he could get to her. He knew it might only be for a very little while, so he meant to make the most of it. Someday, he would break free forever and spend time with her outside of their bed, but for now, he'd take care of her the best way he knew how.

He smiled when he thought of it. On the online applications for the clubs she frequented, Sage wouldn't allow herself to identify as a submissive, so she left the question blank. But she was—she just wasn't ready to admit that out loud to anyone… including herself. He knew once they were together, she would try to top from the bottom as she had in every other relationship she had. All that would get her with him was to be put face down over his knee, getting her bottom spanked bright red for her trouble. They would spend their lives in an eternal dance for power… one they would both enjoy.

He was free. He was naked and hard as he crawled into bed with her. She was lying on her side, hugging a body pillow. Sometimes, depending on her need, he would just spoon her and allow her to sleep in his arms, although his cock never agreed with that decision. It wanted to be in her at all times—her mouth, her ass, but mostly her cunt. She had the sweetest pussy. It produced copious amounts of honey for him to make a meal out of and allowed his cock to breach her easily, sliding in and out smoothly.

Tonight, was not a night for cuddling. Tonight, she needed to be fucked, and he needed to fuck her… desperately. He loosened her hold on the pillow and pushed it onto the floor as he tipped her onto her back. Her thighs parted in invitation without his having to do anything. She needed him, and her body instinctively knew he was there to take care of her. Splayed on her back like the proverbial sacrificial virgin, she was ripe and ready for his use. Inhaling deeply, he smiled. She was incredibly aroused, which made sense since she'd written several sex scenes, although she hadn't completed them. His cock was aching with need.

He rolled over her, parting her legs and hooking

her knees over his elbows. Lifting her hips, he exposed the beautiful, shaved petals of her sex, glistening with her arousal. He ran his tongue over his lips. If she'd finished any of those damn scenes, he might have taken the time to make her come from his tongue before fucking her, but he needed to be inside her. He swirled his cock in her juices to ensure he was well lubricated before slowly, relentlessly, pressing the head of his cock past her entrance into the deepest part of her core.

God, it was all he could do not to come like a first-time schoolboy in short pants. Her pussy was hot and tight as it surrounded his cock, pulsing in harmonic rhythm to the throbbing of his dick. Moaning, she shook her head and writhed as he sank his shaft into her wet heat, pushing forward until he was completely enveloped in her. She moaned again, and he could feel it in his balls. He reveled in the feel of her as he closed his eyes.

He dragged his cock back, her cunt sucking at him, trying to keep him inside. He surged forward with strength and speed. There were times he could hold out, fucking her for hours, but tonight wasn't one of those nights. He hammered her, raw and ferocious in his need. Her hips undulated in his hands as he held her steady. Nothing had ever felt as good as fucking Sage. Nothing.

He changed the angle of his thrusting, so he caught her clit every time he surged forward. Sage cried out as she came, but he held back, wanting to give her at least two orgasms before spending himself in her. He pounded her pussy, grinning as her body stiffened in anticipation of being pushed over the edge into another climax. Her eyes flew open as she came hard a second time, her pussy clamping down on him.

Again and again, he drove into her, hitting the end of her sheath with each thrust. His nerves fired all along his spine as his semen rushed up from his balls and down the length of his cock, spilling into her with the force of a fire hose. He pulled her hard against him, holding her tight as he ground himself against her. Her pussy spasmed, milking his cock for every drop of his seed.

Sage reached for him, and he felt the connection between them vanish in an instant. Once again, he was back inside—trapped, naked and alone.

∽

The next morning, Sage woke, feeling for him beside her but finding nothing. Her phantom lover always left her inordinately satisfied and happy, but with a tinge of bitterness that he wasn't real, and worse than that, she couldn't even conjure him up in her fantasies or dreams. He came to her unbidden when she needed him most or when she was at her most relaxed. They were strange dreams. She could hear the sounds of flesh meeting flesh, hear the sounds of his grunts and groans as he thrust his hard cock into her over and over, and her own moans... but never had a word passed between them, and she couldn't see his face.

She stepped into the shower, getting out just as her breakfast arrived. The waiter entered and set up her breakfast.

"Good morning, Ms. Matthews. I have your breakfast, messages, and mail. Felix..."

"Who's Felix?"

"The head concierge..."

Sage hid her look of shock. The last time she'd checked with the Savoy, the head concierge's name was Richard, who had been with them for years. Felix was the head concierge in the Roark Samuels' novels. Roark lived at the Savoy.

This is weird. What the hell is someone with the same name as a character from my books doing here? Was this some kind of publicity stunt? Had Gail arranged for it? Whatever the case, it was more than a bit disconcerting.

"Have you worked at the Savoy for any length of time?"

"Yes ma'am. I just had my five-year anniversary."

"What happened to Richard?"

"Richard?" the waiter asked.

"Yes, the head concierge."

"I'm afraid I don't know anyone named Richard. Well, that isn't true. I know lots of Richards, but Felix has been the head concierge for longer than I've been here. Corinne came on board as night concierge the same week I was hired."

Sage shook her head. *None of this makes any sense.* She was pretty good at reading people's faces and their body language. She could see no telltale signs of deception. The waiter was telling her the truth. *But how could that be? It was Richard who had supplied her with source material on the hotel and she'd mentioned him in her dedications.*

Ah, that should clear things up, she thought grabbing one of her paperbacks. She looked in the acknowledgements and instead of mentioning Richard, she mentioned Felix. And when she looked through the book itself, Felix had been replaced by another character. Grabbing a different book, she checked again and was astonished to find the same thing.

"Are you all right Ms. Matthews? You look a little pale," said the waiter, solicitously.

"I'm fine. I must be hungrier than I thought."

"Good thing, then, that Felix ordered for you. He had them countermand your publisher's order and sent one of our specialties. Our Arnold Bennett Omelet, as well as the lemon ricotta pancakes, which are extraordinarily delicious, and hash browns with a rasher of bacon, along with a large, freshly squeezed orange juice and Irish breakfast tea."

"That sounds amazing. Way too much and far too many calories, but I'll stab you with a fork if you try to take any of it. I usually don't want much, but this morning, I'm famished," she said trying to sound enthusiastic and covering the feeling that somehow, something in her world had shifted.

"Very good, Miss."

Sage rifled through her messages as she ate. When she'd finished, she went through her mail, leaving the manilla envelope, with only her name and room number, printed by hand, for last.

"Hmm," she said, downing the last of the juice.

She slid the knife under the flap, opening it, and pulled out the thick paper—blank on one side. Sage turned it over and inhaled sharply. The other side was the cover of her yet to be released Roark Samuels' novel. She had revealed it on her private reader page, to the PR firm, and in her newsletter. The picture had been manipulated so her heroine had a gaping slash across her throat, and the hero was holding a bloody knife.

Sage put the picture down on the bed and called down to the front desk, asking them to send someone from security up to her room, then placed a call to Gail.

"Please don't tell me the driver didn't show up," she said.

"No, Gail. The front desk sent up messages and mail with my breakfast. Someone took the cover for Stack of Corpses and manipulated it…"

"Manipulated it how?"

"Put a bloody knife in Roark's hand and made it look like he slit the heroine's throat."

"I'm on my way…"

"No. You handle everyone on that end. Give them my apologies and let the event organizer know what's going on. I've asked the desk to send up someone from security. As soon as they're done with me, I'll head to you."

"Are you sure you don't need me?"

"I am, but thanks, Gail. Someone's at the door…"

"Make sure you check their ID. Call me before you leave."

Gail could be a real pain in the ass, but she did care, and for all her meddling ways, she always made sure Sage was taken care of.

The knock on the door sounded again. Sage put the night latch on and opened the door a crack.

"Can I see your ID, please?"

"Of course, Ms. Matthews," said a gruff voice as he slipped his hotel security identification through the opening. "I'm Gabriel Watson, Gabe, Head of Security here at the Savoy. I have Felix, the head concierge, with me. May we come in? The front desk said you asked for me."

Shutting the door and releasing the night latch, she opened the door, inviting them in. Sage was faced with her second shock of the morning. Felix, the head concierge, stared back at her. A part of her had expected him to look like the character she had described in the book, often being mistaken for Hercule Poirot, but he looked nothing like that. This Felix was a tall man, sleek, lean, but powerfully built, with a small, vertical scar by his left eye, deep brown eyes, sensual mouth, and chestnut brown hair—a far cry from a short, round man with an egg-shaped head and cat-green eyes.

"My dear Ms. Matthews, you look as though someone walked over your grave," Felix said, reaching out for her and leading her to one of the armchairs.

The Roark she had described in her novels was a muscle-bound hunk and contrasted with the soft, round Felix. But here in the real world there was a grace and power to Felix she could feel through his impeccably tailored suit.

"You're Felix."

"Yes, ma'am." Sage reached out and touched his face to assure herself he was real. "Would you like me to call a doctor?"

Sage shook her head, trying to clear the fog from her brain.

"On the bed. It came up with my breakfast… which was delicious. Thank you, Felix."

The Savoy's head of security—a tall man, heavily muscled with the air of someone who could handle himself and any situation that came at him—moved toward the bed. He had shortish blond hair he wore slicked back and icy blue eyes, which somehow seemed warm, set in a face that seemed sculpted from stone.

"I take it the knife and the slashed throat were not part of your original cover art?" Gabe asked.

"No, not at all."

"I can see why you would find this disturbing. Is this the first time you've received something like this?"

"No, back in the States, I have a stalker. It seems he or she has followed me across the Pond."

"How perfectly dreadful for you," Felix sympathized.

"It came in this envelope?" Gabe asked.

Sage nodded again. "You look worried, Mr. Watson."

"Gabe, please. I am. Someone following you across the Atlantic to London isn't a fly-by-night, run-of-the-mill stalker. I'd like to get Scotland Yard involved. Felix and I were part of a Special Ops unit and have a friend there. I'll call him unofficially."

"Thank you."

"In the meantime. I'd like to run a check on your driver before you get in a car with him. I assume you're still going to attend the author event. I'd prefer to take you in my car and give the Four Seasons…"

"How do you know my event is at the Four Seasons?" she asked, beginning to be a bit unnerved by the events of the morning.

"Your publisher, Ms. Vincent, gave Felix a copy of your itinerary and schedule, which Felix gave to his staff and mine. We pride ourselves on the care we give our guests here at the Savoy—especially those with a high profile, who got waylaid by the paparazzi when she arrived at the airport."

"I'm sorry. You're just trying to take care of me, and I'm not being overly helpful," Sage said.

"Gabe and I understand," Felix said, standing. "There's no need to apologize."

"None whatsoever," Gabe added. "When you're ready to come back, I'll have the Four Seasons call me and I'll come get you."

"Thank you. I would appreciate that. If you give me half an hour, I'll be ready."

"I'll be downstairs." Sage watched Felix exit her room and start down the hall. "Gabe?"

"Yes, ma'am?"

"How long has Felix been with the Savoy?"

"Quite some time. He's been here longer than I have. Is there a problem? I can assure you he would never have anything to do with something like this."

"Okay, thank you. I'll be down as quick as I can."

"You take all the time you need." Gabe smiled at her. "I'm at your disposal. I give you my word, you're safe here at the Savoy. Put the night latch on when I leave. Would you prefer I wait for you?"

"Thank you, Gabe. I'm sure I'll be fine."

She closed the door and leaned back against it. Shaking off the feeling of unease, Sage put on her makeup, fixed her hair, and got dressed, then looked at the manuscript on her computer screen. Perhaps she had missed something in looking at the actual books. Sitting down in the chair, she used the search feature to look for 'Felix.' Like the paperbacks she'd checked, the only place the name showed up was in the dedications of the books.

Had she gone mad? She was quite certain she knew what she had written and what she had named her characters and yet, she was being confronted at every turn by what she had thought to be true had changed irrevocably.

If her books had changed so radically, what else was different? She was beginning to feel as though she'd fallen down the proverbial rabbit hole.

CHAPTER 5

Sage met Gabe in the lobby and allowed him to escort her out the rear exit, where he had a car waiting. Pulling into the Four Seasons private entrance and parking the SUV, he escorted her to the ballroom, where she was taking part in a panel discussion.

"I'll give the Four Seasons personnel a heads-up, but I would appreciate if you didn't leave the hotel until I come for you. Stay in the area assigned to your event or in the lobby. Try not to go anywhere alone."

"Gabe, you're starting to scare me," Sage said, only half-joking.

"If I'm only starting, either I'm not doing my job, or you aren't paying attention. My friend at Scotland Yard wants to stop by in the morning if that would work for you."

"I can't believe Scotland Yard is getting involved."

"It's unofficial at this point." Gabe flashed a smile that would melt the panties off most women. "Felix said management at the Savoy is hoping to interest you in extending your stay and participating in the Writer in Residence Program."

"Me?" Sage laughed, inordinately pleased. "They do know what kind of novels I write, don't they?"

"They do. You know what they say, no publicity is bad publicity. Besides, your books are very popular, not only with our staff but with our guests as well. Felix tells me we can't keep your paperbacks in stock, and folks come in all the time, wanting to see the place Roark lives, eats, swims, and… how do I put this…"

"Fucks a lot of women?"

Gabe laughed. "Yes, ma'am. I understand one of the elevators is quite popular with your fans."

"Readers," she corrected automatically. "Thanks again, Gabe."

"You're most welcome, Ms. Matthews."

"Gabe?"

"Ma'am?"

"Sage, please."

"Sage it is. Have a good day and keep your eyes open. If you see anything suspicious or anyone makes you nervous, you head to the front desk or ask for security. Can I see your mobile?" Sage handed him her phone, and he punched in a series of numbers. "My contact info is in there, and I put myself as number five on your speed dial... dead center on your keypad. I keep my phone within reach at all times."

"I wouldn't want to bother you."

"I'd rather you bother me a hundred times than fail to reach out when you're uncomfortable."

"Thank you again, Gabe."

Gail breezed out of the ballroom. "Is everything all right?" she asked.

"Gail Vincent? This is Gabe Watson, the Head of Security at the Savoy. He brought me over here and is going to pick me up at the end of the day."

"Thank you for taking care of my girl," Gail purred.

"Not a problem, Ms. Vincent. Sage, you remember what I said."

"Sage, darling, are you sure you're up to this?"

"Absolutely," Sage replied brightly. "You know me... nothing lifts my spirits or makes me feel better than hanging out with my readers."

"That's my girl. They rearranged the panel discussion so the one that was to follow goes first. Everyone is very concerned about you."

"I'm fine. Let's go. I'll see you this evening, Gabe."

The panel discussion was engaging, and not one question was asked about her stalker. She found herself forgetting about the mutilated cover during the various event sessions.

That evening, Gabe picked her up and escorted her and Gail, who had insisted on coming back to the Savoy with her, back to the hotel and her room. Once inside the hotel, two additional security people joined them. Gabe kept them outside in the hall, with she and Gail sandwiched between he and one of the additional men, while the other swept the room.

"Felix took the liberty of ordering dinner for you, Sage. If you like, Ms. Vincent, I can have them bring something for you as well."

"Thank you. Did you like the Caesar Salad, Sage?"

"I wasn't in the mood for a salad. I had the Shepherd's Pie, and it was excellent."

"Well, I hope they ordered you a salad of some kind for tonight. Sage, dear, you have to watch your weight. I'll have the Caprese Salad," Gail said dismissively.

"Gabe?" Sage asked hopefully.

"No, ma'am. The rib-eye steak, medium rare," he said with a wink.

"You tell Felix he's a good man."

Gail looked at her askance. "Who is this Felix?"

Sage whipped her head around. First, Felix had appeared in the flesh and disappeared out of her manuscript, and now, Gail didn't seem to know who he was. She had to know. They had argued extensively when Sage had given him that name.

"Felix Spenser, the Savoy Head Concierge. He's been very helpful."

"He's not helpful if he's making you fat!" Gail snarled.

"Ms. Matthews, don't listen to her. You have a beautiful figure. Men, at least the ones I know, appreciate a woman with curves. For one thing, they tend to be nicer," Gabe said, shutting down Gail's tirade with a single stare.

Gail harrumphed and turned her back on Gabe.

"Can you teach me to do that?" she asked him, smiling.

"No, ma'am. You are far too nice. Don't let her bully you."

"I won't, and thanks again."

She entered the room and threw the night latch.

"Honestly, Gail, I wish you hadn't been so snooty with Gabe. He, Felix, and the rest of the staff have gone out of their way to take care of me."

"Not helping you stick to a sensible eating plan isn't helpful. If you aren't careful, you'll have to buy a whole new wardrobe."

"It's my money," Sage said with a bit of finality.

Gail continued to harangue her about her eating habits, her wardrobe, her interactions with readers, and meeting, even unofficially, with Scotland Yard.

"If you're going to take the time and be bothered with all of this, we should at least get press coverage," Gail carped.

"I don't want to give whoever it is the publicity. Everything I've read says part of what spurs these people on is seeing their name in the news. I plan to meet with Gabe's friend in the morning, then head over to the event. I'll be on time."

"You weren't this morning."

"I didn't plan on having a threat delivered with my breakfast," Sage said, trying to control her rising temper.

"Maybe just one interview…"

"No, Gail, and that's the end of it. And if you leak the story to the press like you did when I arrived, you and I are going to have a major disagreement."

"Who the fuck do you think you're talking to? You are where you are today because of me…"

"I think my novels had a little to do with it," Sage said sarcastically.

"Not much. I could have taken any two-bit erotic writer and made her into a success. I was trolling an author event when I found you. I could just as easily find another. You were good, raw material. You had the tragic back story of losing your fiancé and your job. Then I added getting you a decent haircut and color, new clothes, and crafted your persona so you appealed to all those love-starved women who find some dominant asshole appealing and voilà—there you are."

"I never knew you felt that way." Sage's anger was threatening to take over. "If you're so sure of that, perhaps you should troll this event and find a replacement."

"Don't think I can't… or I won't!"

Sage stood up, walked to the door, and opened it.

"Please do."

Gail tossed down her napkin, pushed back her chair and stood.

"Don't think I won't."

"I wish you and your new protégé all the success in the world. Don't worry about me at the event. I can handle it. You're welcome to use the return flight ticket, but please ask them to move you so we aren't sitting next to each other. I'll have a letter of dismissal of your services and revocation of our agreement delivered to you in the morning. I'll inform the Four Seasons I will be responsible for your hotel room only as originally agreed, but any extras or anything past the last night of the event is on you."

"Why, you ungrateful little sow! Who the fuck

do you think you are?" Gail screeched, her face turning an ugly shade of red.

Enough, Sage thought. I'm just done. It no longer mattered that they had worked together for so many years. Gail had traded on Sage's sense of loyalty and gratitude for far too long. All the nasty behavior she had tolerated or excused for so many years came to mind, and for once, she didn't feel out of control or powerless. Gail didn't know it, but her mini reign of terror was over. Sage was done making excuses for how Gail treated her; she was about to show Gail that she had some teeth of her own to bare.

Sage drew herself up. "I think I am USA Today, New York Times, and International Best Selling Author Sage Matthews, and if you don't get your skinny, sorry ass out of my room, I will call Gabe and have you escorted from the Savoy."

Gail snatched up her purse and stomped out.

Sage closed the door behind her and sagged against it, waiting to feel as though she had done something wrong, or she was somehow not up to the task she had just set for herself. Surprisingly, it never came. She returned to her meal and finished it, then called down to arrange for breakfast to be delivered to her and was told that Felix had already taken care of it… *of course he had.*

Perhaps she should see if Felix would like to become her personal assistant. He seemed awfully good at taking care of her. Once again it struck her—how the hell had Felix Spenser suddenly appeared in real life? One minute he was a character she had created, and the next, he was here in the flesh and missing from her books… all of them. She'd checked all of her saved manuscripts, and each had contained a head concierge, but none of them named Felix. *What did Gabe have to do with it, if anything?* He seemed to think Felix had been here all along.

The next morning, she was dressed and just finishing her breakfast when there was a knock on the door. She cracked it open to confirm who was on the other side and smiled, opening it wide.

"Good morning, Gabe," Sage said.

"Good morning, Sage. Your cheerful mood this morning appears to be as foul as Ms. Vincent's was last night. Might it be for the same reason?" Gabe asked with a wry grin.

"Would I be a horrible person for saying yes?"

"Not at all," he assured her. "Might I introduce you to my friend and former brother-in-arms, DSI Michael—" He stopped as the blood left her face and her knees threatened to buckle. "Sage, are you all right?"

"Holmes?" she asked, tentatively.

First Felix and now Holmes. What the hell was happening? Was she under so much stress that she was becoming unhinged? Why was she the only one who seemed to notice there were characters from her books showing up in the real world?

"Yes, ma'am. Have we met before?"

Sage shook her head. Standing before her was the exact embodiment of the character of DSI Michael Holmes from the Roark Samuels novels. That would put him close to forty, a bit over six feet with cropped salt-and-pepper hair, with more graying at his temples. She knew he would have a well-muscled body under his conservative suit, a bit brawnier than Felix actually was in real life and a lot more than the way she had described him in the books. If Roark was the character women lusted after and fantasized about, Holmes was the one they all thought they could actually fall for.

She shook her head. "No, just one of those déjà vu moments. It's nice to meet you. I appreciate you taking the time to come."

"It's not a problem. Gabe gave me the envelope and its contents you received yesterday. I'm having a friend in the lab run it through some tests, but I'm not overly hopeful we'll find anything. Might I ask you some questions?"

"Sure? Won't you have a seat? Can I get either of you coffee or tea?"

"Coffee black would be good for both of us," the DSI said.

Of course it would. That's how Holmes took it

in the novels. She'd have to remember to check if he had been replaced as well.

"Do you have any enemies?" Holmes asked.

"I don't know I'd say enemies. My ex-fiancé and soon-to-be ex-publisher aren't overly fond of me, and there are a number of authors who feel I've come too far too fast and haven't paid sufficient dues, but I can't see any of them doing anything like this," she said in all candor.

"I took the liberty of speaking with the Sheriff's Department back where you live, and they are convinced someone is trying to spook you and perhaps has some serious intent. When they heard about the latest incident, they were quite concerned, as am I."

"That's what Gabe thought… if someone was willing to follow me across an ocean, they weren't just doing this for a laugh."

Holmes nodded. "The problem is officially, even if I knew who it was, there's little I could do." Holmes paused and looked at Gabe, who shook his head. "Gabe says I'm wrong and that you aren't capable of doing anything like this. I think he's probably right, but I feel I have to ask; this isn't a publicity stunt, is it?"

Sage sat back, shocked and angry, then slowly stood.

"No, DSI Holmes, it isn't a stunt…"

"Calm down, Sage. Michael had to ask," Gabe said.

"No." Sage shook her head. "I'm not going to calm down. Some wacko is sending me weird and upsetting mail, and I get accused of doing this for fun? Thanks for your help, DSI Holmes. You've fulfilled your obligation to your friend, but you can leave now. I won't trouble you again."

"Sage…" Gabe started.

"Do you think I'm doing this?" Sage asked him.

"No, and neither does Michael, do you?"

"No, I don't, and unless you're an excellent actress, your response to the question settled any doubts I might have had. Please sit down and understand any questions I ask you are ones I'll need to answer for my superiors at the Yard. I think you have a stalker who is escalating. The way the laws are written, there isn't a lot we can do about it… officially, but I can do some nosing around unofficially. I don't think it would be a bad idea for you to hire a security detail."

"I can step up security for you here at the hotel, and I don't mind driving you back and forth to the Four Seasons and speaking to their security people, but I don't know that it's safe for you to wander around London on your own."

"I won't be made a prisoner or recluse by this jerk. I understand what you're saying because it's basically the same thing I was told in the States.

There's little anyone can do without this asshole physically harming me, but he doesn't get to make me his victim. I'd appreciate any help either of you can give me, but I'm not going to hole up in my room in fear," Sage said with some finality. "Now, I need to get to the event."

~

Damn, she was stubborn. Holmes and Felix had managed to pass through the veil and escape. They'd better find a way to help her and keep her safe. All Hallows Eve was just a few days away. The veil between the two planes of existence would be at its thinnest. If he was going to find a way to break free, it had to be then.

Sage approached the laptop and flipped through two different manuscripts. Smart girl. The DSI in her books was no longer named Holmes and bore little resemblance to her description to the original. The expression on her face registered as grim resolution. It was easy to see she knew there was something weird going on. She didn't know what it was yet, but she was determined to find out.

She escorted Holmes and the hotel's head of security to the door—or at least that's what it sounded like. He couldn't see the whole room, but he could hear everything that went on.

He focused on gathering his strength and power.

If he was going to pierce the veil once and for all, it needed to be tomorrow night—with someone stalking Sage, it had become imperative.

~

"He's only trying to help," Gabe said to her once they were in the SUV.

"Really? Hot news flash… accusing me of making this up is not helpful."

"Sage, look at it from his point of view. He doesn't know you. You're an author, and a story like this could bring you a lot of publicity, which would boost your sales."

"I wouldn't do that," she hissed.

"I believe you, but you have to admit, it's been done before. Unofficially, Michael can do some things, but if he really starts to get into it, his superiors are going to want to know he considered all the angles and asked you."

"I suppose so," Sage sighed. "This trip has turned into a bit of a fiasco. Gail and I parted ways, and she's been nasty. I'll call him and apologize."

"Good girl," he said with a smile.

"I should tell you not to be a patronizing ass…"

He chuckled. "But good girls don't say that to people trying to help them."

Sage laughed and enjoyed the warm feeling that spread through her body. Gabriel Watson was good company… and he was right. After he escorted her into the hotel, she dialed the DSI's number and left an apology on his voicemail before focusing on not just getting through, but enjoying the last day. There was a meet the authors' panel discussion this morning, a buffet lunch, then a book signing session.

"What inspired you to become an author?" asked the first person, receiving several answers from different authors.

When it was Sage's turn, she responded, "I was working on an offering to put before the SEC. I was a paralegal in a big, conservative D.C. law firm. I was exhausted and not getting a lot of support from my fiancé. Suddenly, I had this voice inside my head, urging me on and encouraging me to write… thus Roark Samuels was born… and the rest, as they say, is history."

"Sage, do you think you'll ever write anything but Roark Samuels' stories… not that I don't love him, but just kind of wondered."

"Funny you should ask that. I have an idea about a group of wolf-shifters who have the ability to shift at will and don't go through some grotesque metamorphosis. One minute the person is human, the next a wolf."

"Are your stories based upon real-life experiences?" asked an audience member.

"Yes… not all of them mine…" There was

general laughter "I think writers write best when they write about things they know, sharing with readers what something feels like, not only in the physical sense, but in the emotional one as well."

"As a follow-up, I've often heard Jane Austen was quoted as saying she never wrote about a private conversation between two men because she wasn't a man and so had never participated in one."

"I think that's true to some extent, and things were different in Jane Austen's time. But, unlike Jane, I've known a lot of men… some better than others and not all in the biblical sense. I've talked to them, overheard conversations, and asked questions. While I can't speak for others, I can tell you I often run things by those I know who have experienced them before putting them into a book."

"Roark has been known to burn off energy in a kink club. Have you ever been to one, and are you planning to visit any while you're in London?" called a person from the back of the room.

"I have been known to visit kink clubs. For me, they are a safe way to deal with stress and get my needs met without worrying about who I might be meeting and why they might want to meet me. I only frequent clubs with an excellent reputation. I would very much like to visit Baker Street."

The panel discussion broke up, and one of the people in the audience hung back.

"Sage?"

Sage turned. "Hi! Did you want to ask me something?"

"I wondered if you'd ever had any trouble with stalkers. I work here in the hotel, and there's a rumor going around someone's after you. Aren't you afraid?"

Sage sat down on the stage and slid off, closing the distance between them.

"Someone has decided he or she doesn't like my books or me and has made some veiled threats, but I am not about to let any boogeyman—real or imagined—keep me from doing what I love."

"Good for you," she said.

"Are you joining us for lunch?" asked Sage.

"No, it's my day off, and I kind of snuck in here. I just love your books but couldn't afford a ticket. I hoped maybe I'd see you alone and could get you to sign one of them? I have the first one."

Sage linked her arm in the young woman's. "What do you say you join me at my table, then attend the signing? I have an additional ticket and will fix it with the event planner."

"I couldn't…"

Sage grinned. "Sure, you could. Come on."

The smile that broke out across her reader's face reminded Sage why she loved her job. They walked into the dining room, and Sage ensured she had space at her table. She enjoyed those who were seated with her, and there was an animated discussion about authors writing about things they'd never experienced.

"Sage," asked one of those at her table, "who is that blonde who's glaring at you?"

Sage looked to where she indicated and smiled. "That's Gail. She used to be my publisher and handled my marketing and a lot of other things."

"Used to be?" another asked.

"Yes, we had a rather nasty falling out, and I terminated our professional relationship." Sage measured her words.

"Was she mean to you?"

"No, not really. She just didn't want me to write anything other than Roark Samuels novels. I still plan to write them, but I also have a couple of ideas about a paranormal series."

Sage enjoyed a lively and enlightening discussion with her readers, which left her feeling as though she was making the right choice. Later, during the signing, several publishers and agents approached her, slipping their business cards to her and asking for a meeting before she left London or after she returned to the States.

She shook her head. Maybe she should call Gail… try to take back what she had said. They'd done so well together. Sage felt as if she owed Gail something, loyalty perhaps. It had been Gail who had first believed in her; Gail who held her hand through the breakup with Derek and the early years of establishing herself as an author. Perhaps if Gail could see her point of view and agree to give Sage more artistic freedom, they could find their way back to a more equitable and better kind of business relationship. The entire London trip hadn't been a fiasco. All the readers she'd spoken to had been supportive of her ideas for a paranormal series, and Sage had enjoyed not having Gail nag her about what she was eating or drinking.

Sage had finished the signing and was packing up her things when she spied Gail and approached her.

"Gail?"

"The great author speaks. Should I be flattered?"

"Gail, please don't be that way. I thought maybe you'd let me buy you dinner at the Savoy Grill."

Gail looked her up and down as if assessing if she'd put on weight since she'd last seen her.

"Regardless of what you want to do in the future, you have a contract with my firm for your current Roark Samuels' novel. You have a deadline. You don't have time to have dinner with me… or anyone else."

Sage rocked back as if Gail had struck her. She could understand Gail being upset, but the thought they might be able to find a way to work together was squelched—once and for all.

"You were nothing before I found you on that

silly fanfic page and tracked you down at that first signing event, and without me, you'll be nothing again. No one will want to read your books, and I'll blacklist you with every decent publisher, editor, and cover designer I know. You'll rue the day you crossed me," Gail hissed.

"No, but I do regret having thought so highly of you in the past. Obviously, I was mistaken. Take care, Gail."

Sage turned her back and returned to her table to finish packing away her things. While she waited for Gabe, she called the airline and was able to change her ticket to one with an open return, so she and Gail wouldn't have to fly seated next to each other. After some thought, Sage decided to stay a bit longer in London. She then spoke with Felix at the Savoy, who was happy to extend her stay at the hotel.

She slid into the SUV next to Gabe.

"I understand from Felix you'll be staying with us a while longer."

"Yes. I think I'd like to do some sightseeing and absorb some atmosphere. Don't worry, I'm not expecting you to be my personal chauffeur."

"It's not the worst duty I could pull. It would probably be safest if you rehired the limo driver or used cabs as opposed to the bus or the tube."

"I thought, given the location of the Savoy, I'd do a lot of walking."

"Do me a favor and don't go out after dark without an escort. London is a beautiful city and for the most part, pretty safe, but we still have no idea who sent that envelope to you."

"True, but nothing else has happened."

"I know, but still better safe than sorry."

CHAPTER 6

*S*age spent the next few days taking private car tours, arranged by Felix, and walking the immediate area of the Savoy. While at the Tower of London, she struck up a conversation with one of the Yeoman Guard Extraordinary, commonly called Beefeaters. He had offered her a personal tour in the name of research, so she dismissed the driver, tipping him for his service. She was allowed to stay within the Tower walls as they closed down for the evening.

"Shall I call you a cab, Miss?"

"No, thank you. I'm going to grab something to eat, then head back to the hotel. Thank you again for the time you spent with me. I really enjoy having these kinds of details; it makes the setting so much richer and more interesting. I especially loved seeing

Anne Boleyn's grave. Do you ever feel her here at the Tower?"

"They say she haunts Blickling Hall, near Aylsham in Norfolk. But I've always felt her presence here at the Tower on the anniversary of the night before her death. And Hendricks swears he's seen her make her final walk to where the gallows stood. Have a good evening, Miss."

Sage found a local pub and had dinner before heading back to the Savoy. Walking out into the evening, she didn't see any cabs but did see the Tower Hill tube station. *More detail for her books*. She headed to the station and jogged down the steps. The first thing that struck her was how much cleaner it was than the subways she'd been in before. She stood in the middle of the station, observing everything and taking notes. The crowd was bustling; no one seemed to jostle anyone else. The smell of coffee and baked goodies permeated the space, punctuated by the swoosh of the trains as they arrived and departed.

One of the ticket sellers was kind enough to tell her which train and platform she would need to use to get back to the Savoy. The train was pulling into the station when she was shoved violently, stumbling toward the edge of the landing, only barely catching herself before falling. A train station guard grabbed her and pulled her back.

"Careful, Miss. You need to watch where you're

going. If you'd fallen, you could have been badly hurt if not outright killed."

Sage looked behind her but could only see the milling throng of people trying to get to their own destinations.

"I was pushed."

"I very much doubt that. Probably just someone else not watching where they were going."

Not wanting to belabor the point and sound like a crazy American, Sage just nodded, then hopped on the next train heading her way.

"Ms. Matthews," Felix hailed as she entered the Savoy.

"Felix, I thought you agreed to call me Sage… especially since I'm staying here for a while."

"Yes, ma'am, but not in the lobby. It would be unseemly. I'm off duty but was glad to see you come in. We do worry about you. Gabe asked that you give him a call in the morning."

"Will do. Thanks, Felix."

She headed up to her room, took a shower, then settled down to write. Normally, the Roark Samuels novels practically wrote themselves. She had a plot —more of a formula—and could churn out a new book in less than three weeks, but this one just wouldn't come. She'd been trying to get into it for the past week. She had hired a writing coach who had been brutally frank that she needed to take Roark in a different direction—give him more depth and dimension. The coach was insistent that she needed to get at least three or four chapters done.

~

Watching her struggle, he could feel the barrier that divided them weakening and his strength increasing. In the past, when he'd been able to slip his bonds, it had felt as though the veil was filled with holes, and he'd oozed out of a great many of them. But now, when he touched it, it felt spongy and soft, as though it would give way completely.

He knew from Felix that she had extended her stay in London indefinitely. That was good. The longer they were here in the Savoy, the better. He felt closer to her and was better able to keep tabs on her.

Given the way he'd seen the hotel's head of security watching her ass, once he was through, he'd have to make it clear to him that while he appreciated all the man had done for her, Sage Matthews was off-limits.

Holmes had managed to keep the Yard out of it officially but had spoken more than once with the Sheriff's Office in North Carolina. He worried Sage was starting to get too comfortable. If someone meant to do something to her, her inattention could get her hurt… or killed.

"Aaarrrgghhh!" Sage said, pushing away from the desk and standing.

Stretching, she pulled off her robe—she really had the most voluptuous figure. He wanted nothing more than to get his hands on her in the flesh, so to speak. She'd been shopping the day before and had picked up some better lingerie. The bras were fine, but she would soon learn panties were a thing of her past. Grabbing a bra, leggings, and a sweater, Sage got dressed. Had she been at home, she'd have cranked up the music and just danced and sang until she was so tired she could go to sleep or inspiration hit her, which would lead to her writing for several hours. She pulled on her pair of red, LL Bean, fur-lined slippers and headed out of her room.

Where the hell did she think she was going at this time of night?

∽

Sage began wandering the common areas and halls in search of inspiration, finding none.

"Excuse me, Ms. Matthews, may I be of assistance?" the night-time concierge asked, a pretty blonde with long hair she was wearing in a French braid.

Caught up in her own musings, Sage was startled. "No, thanks, Corinne. I just can't sleep, and

Roark's being difficult. I keep hoping if I wander his home turf, so to speak, something will come to me."

"I can't tell you how many of us love your books and Roark. We often think we spot little glimpses of him now and again… as do guests."

Sage laughed. "Really? Like he's haunting the place?"

"Not such a far-fetched idea. The Savoy has several resident ghosts. We like to think Roark would keep us safe from any and all of them if they decided to do anything unseemly. Perhaps if he'd been here, the little girl who haunts the fifth floor wouldn't have died so mysteriously. Then there's the wailing woman. Trudy from the front desk now swears it's because she's done something naughty, and Roark has her over his knee."

Sage laughed as Corinne fell in beside her, escorting her into some of the back areas where guests were normally not allowed. She was finding her excellent company as they meandered through some of the grand halls and rooms of the luxurious hotel.

"Did Richard Harris really live here?"

"Oh, yes, Miss. He had become a favorite of the staff, always a kind word or a way of making people laugh. He was quite sick with Hodgkin's Disease. Felix swears when they wheeled him out on the gurney to the ambulance, he called to the onlookers, 'It was the food! Don't touch the food!'"

Sage laughed.

"We've had several well-known individuals who chose to stay with us permanently and are vaunted for our Writer in Residence program. Have you thought about staying on with us? I know upper management would be thrilled."

"Really?" Sage turned and looked at the young woman, the barest glimmer of an idea beginning to tickle her brain. "Given what I write? I mean, I know the books are popular, but they aren't exactly great literature."

"Says who? They might not be stuffy, but they're fun and exciting, and you always present the hotel in a wonderful light. I overheard one of them say they couldn't buy that kind of good press."

Sage grinned. "Do you think you could arrange that for me? Maybe for the next few months?"

"That would be lovely, and I'd be delighted to help. If you're planning to write, I'll have an ergonomic desk chair brought up to your suite and can arrange for either a larger monitor or an entire desktop computer."

"No, no... I love my laptop's keyboard, but a large monitor would help with the eyestrain. A really comfy chair for writing and a small printer would be great."

"I'll see that they are set up for you tomorrow. What are you working on?"

"I'm trying to finish the last Roark Samuels' novel…"

"Last? Oh, please don't kill him off. If you don't want to write them anymore, at least give him a happy ending…"

"Corinne, haven't you been paying attention? Roark always gets a happy ending," Sage teased.

Corinne giggled. "Right you are and just as he should, but make him fall in love… really in love, and get his own happily ever after. Felix says you've been taking tours. Have you been to the British Museum?"

"Not yet."

"Why don't you let me arrange a personal guided tour while we get your room set up for you? I have a good friend, she's an American. She runs a small, exclusive tour company. If you make a list of what you want to see, I'm sure Rachel can arrange it for you. She often gets people into places no one else can. We'll make the necessary changes to accommodate your personal preferences while you're out. If you make note of what you'd like us to stock in the room for you, we'll ensure you have everything you need."

"That would be wonderful. If I could ask you to not put through Ms. Vincent's calls, I'd be most appreciative."

"That won't be a problem. Felix and Gabe told everyone how nasty she was to you, and we all decided we don't like her. Have you checked your messages? Trudy says word is out you've left Ms. Vincent's firm, and there are several publishers trying to reach you."

"Really?" Sage asked, astonished. "I knew several people heard at the signing event, and I have their cards. I should probably call them, especially those here in Great Britain."

"I think it would be wonderful if your new publisher was here in London. If you like, we can arrange for a secretary or personal assistant, even if you only need him or her for a day or two."

Sage stopped and turned to Corinne. "If you could have the messages sent up with my breakfast and arrange for that tour of the museum while you get my room set up, that would be really helpful."

Corinne grinned. "I would be happy to arrange all of that for you. Any idea how long you'd like to stay with us?"

"Let's say a minimum of three months, then we'll revisit it at two months."

"Very good, Ms. Matthews."

"Please, if I'm going to be staying here, can everybody just call me Sage? Felix has said it would be improper in the lobby, but at two in the morning, Ms. Matthews is awfully formal."

"It would be my pleasure… Sage."

Sage gave her arm a squeeze and headed back to her room, the very beginning of a revised plan for her future starting to take place. A prolonged stay in London would mean letting Charlie and others know so her car and home would be cared for in her absence.

∼

The next morning dawned bright and clear. The words still didn't want to come, but Sage took a shower, then dressed with an energy and lightness of heart she hadn't had for a while. Her breakfast was brought up. She was slowly but surely making her way through the Savoy's menu. She would have to figure a way to do something nice for Felix. He'd taken to ordering for her, and she was rather enjoying just removing cloches to see what he'd had prepared.

As she flipped through her messages, she spotted one from Felix, reminding her Gabe had asked to see her. She grabbed her phone and sent him a quick text, saying she would be available until nine-thirty, then would be out for several hours. His return message said he was on his way in and would see her in approximately thirty minutes.

She reviewed the things sent up from the front desk. The messages from Gail were growing progressively darker and more threatening. She dismissed them, congratulating herself on making the break from her former publisher. There was a message from Gail's boss, asking that she contact him directly, but Sage decided to set that aside since she feared it might be awkward. In addition, she felt as though she owed it to herself to explore all of her options before making a decision.

Good as his word, Gabe knocked precisely thirty-three minutes later.

"You're three minutes late," she said, laughing as she opened the door.

He scowled, as did DSI Holmes.

"And you have been told not to open the door until you know who it is," Gabe scolded.

"Yes, but I'm really not very good at doing what I'm told."

"You're going to have to get better," Holmes added.

Sage was deciding she really didn't like the scowling, albeit sexy, detective from Scotland Yard. She decided she'd never mention him again in one of her manuscripts or better yet, let him get killed off after he didn't take the threat to Roark's latest heroine seriously. Wait… that would be a good idea. If his friend got killed, Roark would feel honor-bound to avenge him or at least solve the case, and Sage could write a heroine who would challenge him and that he could fall for. Maybe Corinne was right. She could give Roark a happily ever after, then do an annual novel with him and the love of his life as a kind of modern-day Nick and Nora Charles, the married detectives from the film noir series.

"Gabe, Felix didn't tell me you were bringing DSI Grumpy Gus. You know, Holmes, I was just thinking I could use you as a great plot device and kill you off in a novel."

Surprisingly, Holmes chuckled. "I'm happy to see you again as well, and at some point in the future, I'm going to rather enjoy seeing you brought to heel by the right man. But that's neither here nor there. As we suspected, there was nothing particularly useful on either the contents of the envelope or the envelope itself. My friend in the lab did say he found some fiber evidence in the self-stick portion of the envelope flap. It looks to be cashmere. If we found the article of clothing it came from, we'd be able to match it, but only circumstantially, but he did say the manipulation of the image was fairly sophisticated, so we're looking—"

"We?" she asked.

"Yes, ma'am. I may not have enough to take to my superiors, but I find the image and the fact that there were no witnesses to how it was delivered—nothing was caught on video—disturbing, to say the least."

"At the risk of having Gabe tsk-tsk me… I rode the tube home from the Tower yesterday evening. I stumbled and had it not been for one of the security people on the platform, I could have been injured."

"Stumbled or shoved?" asked Holmes.

"Initially, I thought I felt someone push me. I was surprised at how crowded it was. But the security person said a local event had just let out and seemed certain I was just jostled."

Gabe shook his head. "Sage, I told you to avoid the tube."

"As I said, doing as I'm told is not my strong suit."

Holmes leveled a look at her. "Perhaps a well-placed swat by a strong hand to your backside would help you to do better."

"You do know, Holmes, that is completely inappropriate."

"Inappropriate perhaps, but I suspect effective if done often enough."

Sage rolled her eyes. "Well, we'll never know, will we?" she challenged.

"I think we'll find out a lot sooner than you think," Holmes rejoined.

"Why do I get the distinct feeling I'm missing something?" Gabe looked back and forth between the two of them. "Had you two met before the other day?"

"Let's just say, Ms. Matthews and I know each other from her books."

Sage stared at him in disbelief... did Holmes

know? How could he? She had written DSI Michael Holmes into the books, but like Felix, he had been replaced by another character she had never written. There was no explanation. Sage remembered the original characters from her books, yet no one else did, and everyone accepted the replacement characters had always been there. She tried to question her sanity or even her memory, but she was quite certain of what she knew, regardless of all evidence to the contrary.

~

She'd been down in the tube? Someone was making threats, and she went down in the tube? He shook his head—she really did need a keeper. No, that wasn't right. She didn't need a keeper who would try to box her in. What she needed was a Dom— someone who would act as her protector, confidant, mentor, anchor, disciplinarian, lover, and dominant —and she would obey and submit whether she liked it or not.

He meant to show her all they could and would be to each other. It was only a question of which she needed more—a sound spanking or a thorough fucking. The best part was the two weren't mutually exclusive, and he meant to have her over his knee and in his bed within short order.

"I understand you're going on a private tour of the British Museum. Try to stay out of trouble," Gabe admonished.

Holmes chuckled again. "I'm tempted to wonder how she could get into trouble at a museum, but somehow, I think Ms. Matthews can pull it off."

Sage grinned, liking Holmes in spite of herself. "I appreciate your faith in me."

"Please, Sage, stay with the guide and allow the town car to take you to and from," Gabe requested.

Sage ushered both men from her room and finished getting ready. When the front desk called up to let her know a driver and guide were waiting at her pleasure, she gathered her things and stepped into the hall.

Sage spent the morning at the British Museum, enjoying both the exhibits and her personal tour guide, Rachel. Once she realized that Sage was more interested in the characters of history than the specific history itself, her entire demeanor changed, and Sage was treated to a lively and engaging waltz through the halls. When the tour was concluded, Sage treated her to lunch at the Great Court Café located in the museum.

Not wanting to take up any more of her time, Sage left after lunch and requested the driver help her see some of the additional tourist spots she had yet to visit. The driver proved to be amenable, and with the Savoy's blessing, treated her to a lively tour of greater London, including some local shops and sites. Sage found time to linger and browse in local vintage and antique shops in the city. She picked up a few items to personalize her hotel room and began considering ways to breathe new life into the Roark Samuels novels.

When she returned, she was greeted by Felix.

"Good afternoon, Sage," he said quietly, stressing her first name. "Corinne spoke with management this morning. As you will be staying with us and have agreed to sell the paperbacks of the Roark Samuels' novels here in the hotel exclusively, we took the liberty to upgrade your room to one of the river view suites… like the one you describe as Roark's residence. We also had an ergonomic chair brought up, as well as a large monitor and small printer." Felix escorted her up to the suite and ushered her in.

"This is the exact suite I was shown the first time I came to the Savoy. I based Roark's suite on it. This is absolutely perfect," Sage said gleefully.

"I'm so glad you're pleased."

"You didn't think I wouldn't be, did you? It's absolutely gorgeous! I may never leave," she teased.

"I don't think there's anyone here at the Savoy

who would think that's a bad idea," Felix said with a smile.

"Felix, could you get me a list of places where I might find some clothes? I had only planned to be here for a week…"

"That's not an issue. All guests have access to our Butler Service. I can have someone meet with you about what you like and can advise you, accompany you, or do your shopping for you."

"Ding! Ding! Ding! I'll take Door Number Three. I am the woman online shopping was meant for." Sage turned and looked at the desk where her laptop, a monitor, and printer had been set up. "The small box next to the monitor?"

"A free-standing hard drive for backup in case you didn't want to use the cloud."

"Thank you, this is just amazing. Please extend my thanks to everyone."

Sage spent the afternoon writing. Thankfully, it was going much better than it had the night before, and she was making excellent progress on the last novel she owed her old publisher. She returned calls to several publishers who had expressed an interest in her work, including mainstream traditional as opposed to erotic romance niche publishers. The most interesting message was from a literary agent and publicist who urged Sage to speak with her before making any decisions about a publisher. Sage returned that call and arranged to meet with her the following week. She wanted a chance to finish the novel, then have a few days off. She thought she might engage Rachel as a personal tour guide to see some of the sites the two had talked about at lunch.

When she reached a good stopping point early in the evening, Sage decided to venture out into the surrounding area and wander along the River Thames until she found a friendly pub. She was mindful of Gabe's words of caution but was determined not to let someone force her to be confined to her room or even to the Savoy.

She entered the dimly lit space, going up to the bar to order.

"Greetings, Mistress. Happy All Hallows Eve to you!" said the bartender, a short, stocky, balding man who had a jovial face and demeanor.

"And the same to you, good sir! What's good?"

"You're an American. Well, welcome indeed!"

Sage reached up and touched the pair of Kirk's Folly witches' shoes that hung from her ears. "It's the earrings, right? That's how you knew I was from the States."

The barkeep laughed. "Yes, ma'am, that was it… nothing to do with the accent. As for what's good, we have a great light micro-brew exclusive to us, and our mac 'n cheese is the best in all of London. It comes with smashed mint peas and bread we make here in the pub."

"Sold! It sounds delicious." The man she

assumed was the proprietor drew her draft. "Is there a place at the bar?"

"Might be down at the end…"

"Hey! Yank! We have room at our table for a pretty girl like you!" called a man from a large round table filled with a number of men and women that looked to be about her age.

She looked at the bartender.

"They're regulars. You'll be safe with them as long as you don't mind a thousand and one questions about America," he said in answer to her unasked question.

"Sounds good. Do I come back for my food?"

"No, we'll bring it out to you."

"Thanks," Sage said over her shoulder as she went to join the raucous table. "Thanks for inviting me," she said, grabbing a seat. "I hate to eat alone."

"What brings you out on All Hallows Eve?" asked the man who had invited her to join them.

"I was at a good stopping place in my work, so I decided to go for a walk and find a place to eat."

"You're from America? I'm Henry, and this is my girl, Darcy."

"I am, indeed," Sage said with a smile. "I'm Sage."

"That's an unusual name," Darcy said. "My favorite author's name is Sage."

"Mine, too," Henry teased. "I always know I'm in for a great weekend when one of Sage Matthews' novels comes out. Darcy thinks I was the model for Roark," he said, striking a pose and making everyone laugh.

"Nope, you're blond, and Roark has dark hair," Sage teased.

"You read Sage Matthews' books? The girls here at the table have a book club and meet once a month."

"Really? That's great. Maybe…"

"Oh my God, Sage? You're Sage Matthews, aren't you?" Darcy asked.

"Guilty as charged," Sage replied with an enormous smile as her food was put in front of her.

Sage spent the evening sharing food and ale and playing darts. At first, there had been a lot of questions about the books, how she got started and the like, but once the novelty wore off, she just became one of the crowd. When a man who also appeared to be on his own entered the now rowdy pub, he was invited to join them and took up a seat next to Sage.

"William Shackelford," he said to the table, shaking Sage's hand. "I'm with the British Foreign and Commonwealth Office."

"Sage Matthews, erotic romance writer."

"Really? That sounds ever so much more fun and exciting than my job."

Sage couldn't remember when she'd had a better time or the last time she'd had so much fun.

A large part of her enjoyment came from the attention she received from William. They seemed to share the same sense of humor. He was sexy and solicitous in the way only a well-raised English gentleman could be. As the evening went on, he found ways to subtly touch her. When she didn't dissuade him, the touches got bolder—a glancing touch along her breast, a caressing hand on her backside. Gradually, his gentle fondling ignited the spark of her arousal into a flame that grew brighter with each passing hour. While she had enjoyed pleasuring herself and the often-sensual dreams she experienced at night, it had been a while since Derek's departure from her life and she hadn't had a chance to visit any of the clubs she enjoyed in a while.

William drew her hand beneath the table and placed it on his thigh, allowing her to decide for herself whether to leave it there or move it to feel his thick, hard cock. Sage leaned into his body, and William wrapped his arm around her as she slid her hand down, covering his cock and giving it a gentle squeeze.

"Mmm... that's nice, love," he whispered in her ear.

She grinned and nuzzled him. "Yes, it is."

They continued to play darts with their newfound friends. The only difference was as the evening wore on, William pulled an unprotesting

Sage into his lap between turns at the throw line. She found herself relaxing back into his body, his arm curling around her waist, and his hand resting lightly between her legs. She could feel his cock throbbing beneath her, promising all kinds of pleasure to be had.

More than a little tipsy, those at the table called the evening to a close. Sage left the pub with William and offered no resistance, or even protest, when he pulled her into an alleyway, pressing her against the brick wall and kissing her. William took the lead, his mouth covering hers, his tongue darting out to trace the seam of her lips as his hands moved from her shoulders down her back to cup her buttocks and bring her closer. Sage's lips opened and his tongue surged into her mouth—tasting, exploring, devouring.

When he suggested a walk, Sage's only protest was leaving the shelter of the alley and William's arms. William drew her hand through the crook in his arm, and they walked several blocks along the Thames. Although it was late fall, the weather was mild, and she was enjoying the night and the company more than she had anything in a very long time.

Earlier in the week, she had feared her trip to London was turning into a fiasco, but little by little, she seemed to be finding her way and making it a triumph. Everything about the city seemed to have a positive impact on her life. She and William walked hand-in-hand in companionable silence as Sage mused that, as an author, she was in a position to pursue her career anywhere in the world… including London, perhaps even with William.

CHAPTER 7

Most of the wide causeway they meandered down was well lit, but William drew her into his arms, ducking into the shadows and behind trees, his hands brazenly roaming her back and buttocks, pressing his hard length against her body. She could feel his shaft pressing through his trousers, straining to get to the place between her legs. Never tarrying long, he moved them along the walkway until they came to one of the few bridges that crossed the river. Sage noticed there was no one around.

He turned her into the darkness and kissed her again. She ran her hands down his arms, well-muscled under his perfectly cut suit. Sage nibbled kisses along his strong, square-cut jaw, enjoying his clean and masculine scent.

William drew her hand down so there could be

no question in her mind he wanted her. His cock pressed against the front of his trousers, trying to get out. Sage enjoyed fondling him, feeling his size and strength, wondering what it would be like to have him lie between her legs before he surged forward, driving into her, stroking her to ecstasy. She could feel desire pooling between her legs and realized she was looking forward to being pleasured with something far better than any vibrator.

"Why is it women like to wear leggings?" William whispered seductively, cupping her bottom before running his hand inside her waistband and beneath her panties to caress her bare flesh.

Sage moaned and might have protested, but William's mouth captured hers in a searing kiss, overwhelming her already frayed senses. How long had it been since she'd been kissed like this? Had she ever? She melted against him, her body molding to his as she groaned in need. His lips rubbed against hers, and hers parted, inviting his tongue to taste her more deeply, entreating and emboldening him. Sage knew it was madness, but didn't care when he pushed her leggings and panties down past her buttocks, exposing her mons and lower body to the cool London night.

He gripped the nape of her neck with one hand, holding her in place, while he leaned her back against the stone pillar of the bridge support. He used his other hand to find the soft curls at the apex of her thighs, gently trailing his fingers between them until he discovered her clit, circling and tugging before pressing it firmly as if it were some kind of ignition button, which it seemed to be. Sage felt dizzy with need, clinging to William while he explored her most feminine place.

"Wanton little wench, aren't you?" he whispered.

"Not usually," she said with a muffled laugh. "I think all that ale has gone to my head."

William spun her away from him so she was facing the wall, her hands splayed on the damp stone. He stroked the cleft between her butt cheeks, circling her dark rosebud before slipping his hand between her legs and penetrating her wet heat with two fingers, plunging them in and out.

"William," she breathed.

"Shh, Sage," he crooned, fingering her while stroking her hair before drifting his hand to her breast and squeezing it briefly before dipping into the pocket of his jacket. "If I'd known you'd be this ready for a good romp, I might have set this up differently."

The seductive tone was gone—in its place was one as cold as ice.

Sage felt the thin, cloth-covered wire slip around her neck as he removed his fingers from her pussy and grasped the other end of the garrote. William used his hard thighs to force her against the stone as she brought her hands up to try to keep him from strangling her.

"Why?" she barely managed to stammer.

"Why not?" he hissed.

The loop tightened and her breath was cut off as darkness began to cloud her mind. She tried to struggle, to no avail. She felt cheated when her life didn't flash before her eyes. She wondered why she had been able to provide her readers with a storybook hero... yet failed to find her own. All she felt was the peace of acceptance as the noose cut off her air. Time and space shimmered and seemed to shift, darkness descending upon her.

Just before she lost consciousness, she thought she heard a spitting sound... then the blackness became complete.

∼

The room was dark, lit only by the ambient light through the windows. All he could see was what was directly opposite the veil. Where the hell was she? Hadn't she heard both Gabe and Holmes tell her to take care with her safety? It was late, and she had yet to return. He pressed against the barrier that separated them and felt it give way—more than the usual permeable feeling, more even than the spongy texture that had been gaining in the last few days.

Without warning, he could feel a loop tightening around Sage's lovely neck. Her airway was being closed, and she couldn't breathe. Her hands clawed at her throat, but the noose was too tight. Someone was trying to kill her, and if he couldn't break through, the assassin would succeed.

That was not happening.

He leaned his shoulder into the barrier and shoved with all his might. The veil gave way, and he felt himself falling forwards, tumbling through time and space as everything around him shimmered. When he landed, instinct took over, and he rolled to his feet. Looking around, he realized he wasn't in her hotel room. It took only a moment to recognize he was outside the Savoy, not far away, but down by one of the bridges that crossed the Thames. He knew she was ahead in the shadow of the bridge, out of the sight of prying eyes.

Running toward her, he prayed to whatever power had allowed him through the veil that he wouldn't be too late. He could feel unconsciousness descending on her. He was running out of time. He strained his eyes to pierce the darkness and finally located them. Sage was shoved up against a wall, her killer's thighs pressing her tightly against it as he leaned back, the handles of the garrote firmly in his grip. He stopped, reaching into the pocket of his tuxedo jacket, praying his SIG Sauer was there. Thank God it was, as was the silencer that had been made to his specifications to seamlessly fit his gun.

Checking to ensure it was loaded and the safety was off, he stopped and took aim.

Squeezing the trigger—in the same way he would later squeeze her nipple or her clit—the SIG responded in the same way, doing precisely as he wanted, the sound of the two bullets making no more than a quiet spitting sound. The first caught the assassin in the side of the head, his hands loosening their hold as the impact spun the killer toward him, the second bullet catching him between the eyes.

He ran forward, pocketing his gun as Sage slid down the wall. He ran to her, sliding to try to catch her before she hit the dirt. She couldn't be dead… not his Sage. He'd come too far, endured too much to be with her. He would not allow her to die. He'd made love to her in her dreams just the night before. Now, when he was so close, he would not allow her to leave him. She was his, and he would have her.

"Don't you die on me, Sage. Come back, do you hear me? Holmes was right, you know, you need someone to look after you, but I'm here, love. Your Master is here."

After what seemed like an interminable amount of time, he saw her chest rise and fall—slowly at first, then more steadily as she gasped for air. He dragged her into his arms. He had to get her back to the Savoy. He gently pulled her leggings back up and placed her on her side for just a moment as he rifled through the man's pockets. No ID—no surprise there. He had a large roll of bills and nothing else. He pocketed the money and rolled the body over the edge into the icy water before returning to Sage.

Cradling her to his chest, he stood and came out of the darkness from under the bridge. He scanned the area, finding no one around. He got his bearings and began walking back to the Savoy, carrying her as if her weight was nothing. He slipped in the back entrance, using the key card in Sage's purse, accessing the elevator, and finally entering her room. He stripped her and pulled back the covers of the bed, laying her gently on her back, then retrieved a cold, wet washcloth from the bath and pressed it against the growing weal.

He called down to the front desk and asked that ice be brought to the room. He waited by the door, gun readily available in his pocket, answering just as there was a knock.

"Good evening, Mr. Samuels. Would you like me to set this up?" the butler asked.

"No, thank you, Simmons. I can take it from here. Would you please cancel the alarm or breakfast Ms. Matthews had arranged for tomorrow? I'm afraid she overindulged, and I'd like to let her sleep in. Once she's awake, we'll see how she's feeling and take it from there."

"Very good, Sir."

He closed the door, locked it, then turned back to Sage. She was a vision lying sprawled on her back, her auburn hair splayed out all around her. He grinned. He really was a rotten bastard. She'd almost died, and all he could think about was getting her healed and fucking her silly. He looked at the soft curls nestling at the apex of her thighs. He'd take care of that in the next day or two. He wanted her bare and available for his use whenever he wanted her.

He wrapped the wet washcloth around several ice cubes and pressed it against her neck. She started to fuss but quieted when he soothed her. Once she was settled and sleeping, he used her mobile and called Holmes.

"You're through… for good?" the DSI answered.

"What made you think it was me?" he asked.

"Had to be you. That's Sage's mobile number, and she doesn't have mine." He chuckled. "If you're calling me, either you're losing your touch, or you've worn the poor girl out."

"Neither. You fucked up, Holmes. Someone tried to kill her and damn near succeeded."

"What?" The DSI's tone changed from bantering to serious and concerned in an instant.

"I was drawn to a place under a bridge. There was a man with a garrote around her neck. I put two bullets in him, then dumped the body in the Thames."

"Are the two of you all right? Does she need medical assistance?"

"Her throat is bruised, but nothing I can't handle. The oddest thing… they moved her to the room she used as the basis for my lodgings here at the Savoy. I called down to the Butler Service here in the hotel and asked for ice. When the guy came to the door, he greeted me by name. Interesting thing is, I knew his as well. Do me a favor and call Felix in the morning. Let him know what's happened, and that Sage and I are not to be disturbed."

"Are you feeling any pull to go back behind the veil?"

"None at all. In fact, the longer I'm here, the stronger I feel in general. Don't worry about it, Holmes. We'll figure it out… Is it odd to be walking around?

"At first, but the feeling fades, and being here feels normal as though I've always been here. At first, I worried about somehow being sucked back without warning… especially the first time I was intimate with a woman, but even that concern has lessened."

"Good to know. It'll be good to see you and Felix. What about the security guy?"

"Gabe? He's a good man… very concerned

about your girl. He knew there wasn't enough to get me officially involved but also knew this was beyond his ability to figure it out and keep her safe, so he called me in unofficially. Just like everyone else, he seems to accept we've always been here. It's the oddest feeling, not just that they know you... you know them too and not just their names. The first time I walked into the Yard, it felt as though I'd always been there. People greeted me by name, and I knew all of theirs as well. You take care of your girl. I'll figure out how to retrieve the body, then we'll try to figure this thing out."

He ended the mobile call and smiled as he watched her sleeping. She'd rolled over on her side and was curled with a pillow snug against her body. She wasn't going to need that in the future, either.

Now, what to do with her? He'd wanted her for so long and didn't intend to waste any time establishing their relationship. She needed to learn from the get-go just which one of them was in charge— and it wasn't her. He grinned. He knew just the thing to bring that point home. He looked in the bedside drawer and his smile grew broader. Next to the little pouch, where she kept her sex toys, was the kit containing his. He was reasonably sure what it would contain and also that she had never had one used on her.

He opened the kit and pulled out his prize, a simple silver butt plug. Shiny and sleek, it shouldn't be too large for her to handle. He stroked the crevice of her ass, rimming her dark rosette. Asleep, it was relaxed and gave to the light pressure of his finger. He was quite certain he would be the only man to ever have her ass. She'd been squeamish about incorporating anal sex into her books, but had finally relented when her editor insisted.

Checking his kit, he decided—although she had been naughty, recklessly going off with some assassin and letting him pull her leggings and panties down—it didn't rise to the level of using peppermint lube on the plug for her first time. He spread the regular lube over it, looking at her tight little hole. His cock hardened at the thought of that petite ring of muscle all but strangling his cock as he pressed into her in the future.

Teasing the plug against the tight ring of muscle, he inserted the tip and watched her dark rosette fight to keep him out, but it wouldn't win… he would; he would win everything. He twisted the handle, wedging the tip in and gently pushing, drawing it back before pushing it back in. He repeated the action over and over until finally it was seated. There, that ought to give her something to think about.

∽

The inky darkness which had shrouded her began to recede. Her eyes fluttered open as consciousness returned, and she woke. At first, Sage was frightened. Someone had tried to kill her—not someone, William Shackelford. Why? The fear retreated as she realized she was safe in her bed at the Savoy. What had happened? How had she gotten here? She reached for her throat.

"There shouldn't be any scarring, if that's what worries you," a cultured British voice said—deep, decidedly male, seductive, and posh. "Although that should be the least of your concerns. How are you feeling? Are you all right?"

Sage glanced around her surroundings, her eyes fixing on the tall, muscular man who stood looking at her like some dark guardian angel. He was gorgeous. Even standing still, there was an energy about him that made him look like a large predatory beast, ready to strike at any minute. He wasn't just tall, but brawny, with not an ounce of fat—all lean muscle and sinew. The question about what it might feel like to be trapped beneath him flitted across her mind. Sage could feel desire begin to pool between her legs.

Who was he?

She was back in her hotel room at the Savoy, that much was apparent. Whoever the gorgeous hunk was, he looked perfectly at ease. It was still dark out. What was he doing in her room?

"Wh-Who are you? Wh-What are you doing in my room?"

"That's not how this works, Sage," he rumbled. She noticed his lips had a decidedly sensual shape. "I'm the one who did the rescuing, which means I'm the one who asks the questions. I asked how you were feeling and if you were all right."

As Sage became more awake, her current circumstances were revealed in greater detail. She was in her room at the Savoy with a man she didn't know but who felt oddly familiar. Someone—William—had tried to kill her after she had allowed him to feel her up and strip her leggings and panties down around her knees. The thought of having been found like that caused her to blush, which led her to her next revelation.

She was naked, and he seemed well aware that she was. The dampness she could feel gathering at the entrance to her core was accompanied by her nipples tightening and becoming uncomfortably stiff, and it felt like there was something stuck up her bum. She started to reach around to feel for the offending object.

"Ah, ah, Sage, leave that alone. You've been very naughty, and brats who misbehave sometimes have reminders to behave put up their bottom hole."

"What the fuck? Who do you think you are?" Sage snapped, outraged.

"That's enough, Sage. I must say, for such an intelligent and articulate author, you do use the most vulgar language. That really needs to end."

Sage rolled to the other side of the bed and onto her hip, facing away from him, and again stretched her hand back around to remove the butt plug. The more awake she became, the more uncomfortable it was. He moved silently, but the crack that resounded as his hand connected with her bare bottom was as clearly audible as her yowled response.

"I told you to leave that alone. The plug stays where it is until I decide to remove it. Given your writing, I was a bit surprised you were so tight back there. I would have thought you might have at least tried it. You have an excellent imagination, and I always found your descriptions of the sensations, as well as the emotions associated with it, spot on. Or rather what I imagine a woman feels when she gets her bottom hole plugged. It might be a bit uncomfortable, but it will get less so with time and repeated use. We'll need to work on that. At some point, I'm going to fuck your ass… and I'll want you to enjoy it."

Sage rolled off the bed, bringing the sheet with her, and faced him. The plug provided pressure to her bottom and felt odd but disturbingly pleasurable.

"I don't know who the fuck you think you are..." she said, her breathing a bit thready and uneven.

"That is enough, Sage. I had thought you might offer some explanation for your behavior last night. I understand wanting to go out and experience the real London, but did you seriously consider the repercussions of getting drunk in an international city and wandering off with some bloke you just met? Or what a field day the press would have had if someone had photographed you as some guy fucked you up against a wall? The fact that your would-be suitor was actually an assassin and would have left you stripped half-naked to be found tomorrow morning? That was just stupid, and you are far from stupid."

Sage started to take a step toward the bathroom door, where hopefully, there'd be a phone. She could lock herself in and call for help. The only problem was when she moved, the plug sent a jolt of pure sexual need coursing through her system... staggering her.

The stranger stepped between Sage and the door to the bath, almost as though he knew what she was thinking... and feeling. He flicked on the lamp beside him, its light revealing he was dressed all in black—boots, jeans, belt, and a t-shirt that seemed molded to his body. The determined look in his eye told her she had no chance of getting by him. She refused to be cowed—aroused maybe, but not intimidated. Her spine straightened, but her knees threatened to buckle, and the pulsing in her nether region caused her to retreat.

He came around the end of the bed and made his way toward her, moving the same way a feral cat plays with a mouse, but he was far more predatory than any domesticated cat. There was a powerful grace that exuded "alpha male" with every step he took.

"Where is it, precisely, you think you are going, love?" he purred with the smallest indication of seductiveness.

"I'm the aggrieved party in this…"

"The aggrieved party? Hardly," he snorted. "What you are is a brat who needs to get her bottom spanked, well and often. You need to understand, from this point forward, you are not going to engage in foolish, dangerous behavior… at least, not without serious consequences."

"Excuse me?" she drawled.

The large, panther-like male took a deep breath and sighed. "Don't play coy with me, Sage. It's high time you were given a set of rules by someone who will hold you accountable."

"Rules?" she squeaked.

Why wouldn't he stop stalking her? Why did he have to get so close? Couldn't he see she was having trouble breathing? And how had she become comfortable with something stuck up her ass, so all she felt when it moved was pure pleasure and surging arousal?

"Yes, rules. You ought to be grateful I think it's only fair you know what those rules are before I punish you when you break them." He chuckled—a deep, melodious sound. "Given your rebellious nature, I'm sure you will break them on a fairly routine basis. While your Master isn't going to like it when you break the rules, the idea of spanking that pretty bottom of yours is quite arousing."

"Master?"

Rules? Master?

Sage felt her sheath quiver in exaggerated anticipation, her nipples beaded to the point of pain, and her clit pulsed… hard. Her entire body shuddered as a precursor to an orgasm. *Was he crazy? Was she dead? Was this her version of heaven or hell?*

"I prefer you refer to me as Sir or Master, especially when you are being chastised. I'm not very happy with your behavior earlier this evening. For one, as I said, it was stupid. Two, your Dom doesn't share his girl… unless she's been very naughty, and he feels she needs a more intensive lesson in submission."

This wasn't making any kind of sense. She didn't write D/s books. *Who the hell was this guy?*

"What kind of whack job are you?" she snarled, her anger pushing past her arousal, but fueling it nonetheless.

"The first rule—you will speak to me respectfully and truthfully. Any deviation from compliance will result in a soaped mouth and a spanked bottom. Rule two—when we are alone, you will refer to me as Sir or Master. Rule three—you will not put yourself in danger. Rule four—you will mind me at all times. Let me stress the importance of rules three and four. Penalties for breaking either of them will not be pleasant. I think the rules are pretty simple and straight forward. Do you need me to write them down?"

"No, I don't need you to write them down," she said quietly before reminding herself she didn't answer to this man, and indignation reared its ugly head. "I don't know who you think you are or why you think I'm going to do what you say, but I can assure you that you are wrong. Now get out, or I'm calling security."

"And what is it you think Gabe Watson would do? I assure you he is not a man given to interfering between a man and his woman. Make no mistake… you are mine. As to who do I think I am? I think I am who you created me to be."

"What the fuck do you mean by that?"

He shook his head. "And that, Sage, is a bridge too far," he said, snatching the sheet away.

He was on her in the blink of an eye. The stranger fisted her hair and marched her into the large bath off the bedroom. She clawed at his hand but couldn't shake it loose. Before she could process what he was about, he turned on the faucet, adjusted the temperature, and soaped up his hand. Pressing her against the vanity, he exposed her dark passage with the butt plug lodged inside. The stranger released her hair, grasped the handle of the plug and pulled it free.

Arousal coursed through her system, making her gasp. Taking advantage of her opened mouth, he kept her jaws from closing, quickly and efficiently soaping the inside of her mouth, covering her cheeks, tongue, and teeth. When he was finished, he handed her a small glass of water, barely enough to rinse her mouth.

Before turning off the tap, he washed the butt plug and his hands, then dragged her back out into the sitting room. Sitting down on the sofa, the outline of a large, bulging, throbbing cock was clearly visible. She hardly had time to notice it before finding herself face down over his knee, feeling it pulse beneath her belly.

His hand descended in the first of many hard strikes to her bottom. Sage wailed in pain and outrage, but the stranger didn't seem to notice, merely beginning a strong, steady tempo of harsh blows with his open palm. She tried to wriggle her way off his lap, but he held her fast and rained down swats that covered her backside in a wave of ever-increasing misery.

Although Sage had become known for a hero who routinely spanked the women he was intimate with, she had personally never experienced a spanking. Oh sure, she went to clubs and found being bound to a St. Andrews Cross and flogged relieved her stress and increased her libido, but she had always thought being spanked, especially over a man's knee, was too intimate, and she was right. This was arousing, intoxicating, insane, and painful. She had never felt the heat and agony that spread across her ass as a result of his discipline. Most interesting was the sense of peace and contentment that came with it, as if she was being enveloped in a soft, fuzzy blanket—but that was between strikes. Every time his hand landed on her bottom, all she felt was pain.

"Shit, you bastard, that hurts," she wailed.

"So, my girl needs her mouth washed out with soap again so soon? I suppose I was too generous letting you rinse. I won't make that mistake again," he calmly declared, still tattooing his displeasure all over her buttocks.

Sage gritted her teeth, then bit her lip—anything to keep him from knowing he was getting the better of her. She couldn't believe the level of torment involved in getting spanked. The heroines in her books always stoically endured, at least until the hero used his belt or a strap. Her backside wasn't the only thing that hurt. Her nipples had become so stiff, they begged for his attention, preferably not gentle. Her pussy literally ached to feel him inside her, thrusting in and out, stretching her inner walls, and riding her until she couldn't walk. It felt like electricity played all across her skin, seeping into her pores to race through her entire system.

The spanking stopped, but before she could process what had happened, the stranger pried apart her legs and used two fingers to penetrate her, roughly fingering her until she came, screaming and writhing on his lap.

Oh my God, please tell me I didn't just climax from this guy's treatment of me! Wishing was no use—she sure as hell had. She collapsed against him.

Sage allowed the stranger to help her stand, then steady her when her legs threatened to give way. She wished to God she wasn't stripped naked —with beaded nipples, flushed skin, and a pussy still reverberating from the power of her orgasm. He acted as if he hadn't just beat her ass, then caused her to climax from his rough fingering.

"Now, Sage, go put your nose in the corner by the fireplace," he said calmly.

"I won't," she managed to say.

"You will, or you'll get your first taste of leather. Does your Master need to add a set of stripes to your very red bottom?"

Master? Where was he getting this? Didn't he

know she didn't write D/s books? She wrote straight-up erotic romantic suspense with a heavy dose of action and adventure. How did this clown get off calling her his girl or love and insisting she call him Sir or Master? That was so not happening… but it was, leaving in its aftermath a surge of arousal that pulsed and quivered throughout her being.

Sage couldn't quell the trembling that originated in her nether region, ran up her spine, and branched off along her nervous system. Her toes curled, and her body tensed in anticipation. She wanted and needed him in a way she couldn't comprehend. She wanted to feel his hands exploring and touching her body, not with tender caresses, but with tugging and pinching. More than that, she wanted to feel the sizeable bulge trapped in his pants.

She wanted him to shove it inside her, powerfully thrusting in and out until she came again. His cock pushed and strained hard against his fly. She wanted to see it set free so he could part her thighs with his own and ram it to the end of her sheath. As bad as the realization was that she craved his less than gentle touch, she feared this first spanking was much like the first taste of cocaine—igniting a need for more, which would be hard to resist.

She tried to remind herself she was the victim. William, if that was even his name, had tried to garrote her. *Why? What happened when she blacked out? Who was this guy, and why did he think he had a right to spank her? Why did it feel so right that he had?*

Sage had taken care of herself for a long time. With the exception of putting up with Gail, she never backed down, ever, and she wasn't about to start now. Why then, couldn't she hold his steely gaze? Her emotional and physical responses were all over the place. One minute her stomach was so tied up in knots, she thought she might throw up. The next, it danced all over the place in gleeful relief that at last, someone had figured her out, seen through her façade. Sage knew to hold his gaze was to offer him the proverbial window to her soul. He would be able to read all her thoughts and emotions, all her needs and secrets.

She watched him reach to unbuckle his belt. The pulse between her legs increased, beating so hard, she was surprised he couldn't hear it.

"Now, Sage, or your first kiss won't be from your Master's lips but from his belt."

He took her by the shoulders and turned her toward the corner, gently nudging her in the direction of the fireplace. When she hesitated, he patted her backside gently, but the unvoiced threat was palpable. She winced but went where he directed her.

"Who are you?" she whispered, more to herself than to him.

CHAPTER 8

Who was he? How could she not know that? She had given him life, although she might be regretting that right now, but she hadn't given him agency—that and his freedom, he'd taken for himself.

He was used to watching Sage's train wreck of a life play out as she wrote her novels. Granted, he could only see what was right in front of the laptop when it was open, but it was enough. He only had glimpses of the events that influenced her life but was able to see the effects and aftermaths. He had tried repeatedly to get her to let him deal with the heroines of her novels in a more meaningful way. Sage had consistently written them as silly shills for herself. He'd wanted to keep them safe and help them to flourish and grow. Instead, she'd made each one a self-contained story that never allowed her hero or heroine to evolve.

In each novel, a woman found herself in peril. Roark would come in, at the behest of some person who professed to care for her, then become annoyed with the heroine so he could justify spanking and fucking her. The result had become predictable; the lady in question always fell in love with him. Then inexplicably, she would escape his watchful eye, and he'd have to save her before spanking and fucking her again. Then instead of letting the relationship expand to any kind of meaningful conclusion, Sage would have him merely drop her off with her father, fiancé, or dreary little life before he returned to his suite in the Savoy. Nice touch. The way she wrote Roark, he really was a bastard.

What Sage failed to realize was there was so much more to him… there could be so much more between them. Sage needed a loving dominant, someone who could see to all her needs—structure and support for boundaries and consequences, as well as those for pleasure and pain. Sage would be quick to tell anyone she wasn't into pain for pain's sake. She had just enough of a touch of masochism that pain freed her from her self-imposed limitations and rigidity. What she needed was to know there was someone who cared enough about her to hold her accountable and see that she behaved in the best ways possible to achieve her goals and dreams.

And pleasure… he smiled, his cock growing hard. There was a deep well of pleasure in Sage no one had guessed existed. He meant to explore her hedonistic need for erotic and sensual stimulation and satisfaction. His girl was a proverbial alley cat in heat when it came to sex. She'd almost let her assassin fuck her before he killed her. He might be her tomcat, and he might well fuck her under a bridge sometime, but by Christ, it would mean something to her, and she would stay safe.

It was difficult to see only the parts of her life visible from the laptop or the pages of her manuscript—either on the printed page or from her screen. In the past, all he could do was observe what was directly in front of him or hear what was going on in the same room, occasionally eluding the bonds she had created to invade her dreams. He could touch her and have sex with her, but had never found a way to pull her over his knee to administer a spanking when she needed one. He hadn't been able to escape his prison on the written page for any length of time.

Last night had been different…

As usual, he'd been imprisoned in Sage's laptop. He'd felt uneasy when she hadn't returned before dark. He'd begun casting about—sifting through emails, linking up with the Savoy's vast computer network—anything that might reveal her whereabouts.

He'd all but given up when he felt her presence, stronger than he ever had in the past, and looked up, expecting only darkness. She had closed the computer before she'd taken a shower. Pity that… he did enjoy seeing her naked—voluptuous curves, beautiful auburn hair, and eyes the color of a soft, summer sea. Instead, he saw Sage's room, which meant someone had been in her room and opened her laptop.

Someone had tried to access the system but failed. All he could see was the room and couldn't hear anything. He started to turn away when the room began fading into a shimmering soft focus, and he wondered if the battery was dying. Roark tried looking through what appeared to be gathering fog.

Suddenly, two figures came into sharp relief—Sage with her leggings and panties pulled down past her knees, pressed up against the wall of a bridge support, and some guy fondling her. Who was this guy, and why was Sage allowing him to have what should have always been his? What was he getting from his jacket pocket? If Roark had her half-naked and willing, he damn sure would not have been fumbling in his pocket. What the bloody hell! The man had a garrote!

"Sage! Pay attention! That wanker is going to kill you!" he'd shouted as he began to test the strength of the barrier that divided them.

She didn't hear his warning. The would-be assassin now had a handle in each hand and was pulling the noose tight. She brought her hands up to try to ward off her own strangulation but appeared to be too late. He could feel her life ebbing away, then heard her desperate plea for a hero of her own. Who better than the one she had created?

No sooner had the words formed in his mind, than he felt the barrier begin to soften. His resolve to get to her hardening, he'd shouldered his way through. The veil had given way, and he charged through, tumbling in a void until he'd been transported to the walkway not far from Sage and her assailant. He'd rushed toward the struggling pair, reaching into his pocket and finding his favorite SIG Sauer, his silencer already attached. Taking aim, he'd fired twice, hitting the man once in the temple and once between the eyes when the force of the first bullet spun him away from Sage to face Roark. Putting on an extra burst of speed and sliding under her like an American ballplayer at third base, he'd been able to keep her from hitting the ground. He disposed of the body before bringing her back to the Savoy.

Surprised to find she had the keycard to his fictional suite, he took her inside, ostensibly to ensure she hadn't been hurt, but even Sage wouldn't have written such a silly scene. It was a setup for a sex and punishment scene if ever there had been one—one he intended to take full advantage of.

Roark had no intention of passing up the opportunity to get his hands on her naked flesh. God's teeth, she felt good, her skin smooth and delicate to the touch. He caressed her beautiful bottom and thought again how good it would look stained with his handprints, but to give her the spanking she needed, he had to wait until she was awake. He wanted her to know she was being spanked and why.

Then he remembered a scene she'd added to the third Roark Samuels novels. Roark liked anal sex, especially with arrogant women who needed a comeuppance. He chuckled when he opened the nightstand drawer to find his kit containing a set of graduated butt plugs as well as two kinds of lubricant—one a straight lube, the other with peppermint extract that could give Sage's bottom hole something extra to think about. He opted for the first and had very gently worked the smallest of the plugs past the ring of muscle guarding her dark entrance.

Now here they were—Sage's nose pressed to the corner and her question hanging in the air between them.

"Who am I? As I said previously, brats are not the ones who ask the questions, and you, love, have yet to answer mine. The two most pressing ones are, first—what were you thinking, getting drunk and wandering the streets of London with someone you didn't know? And second—who would want to kill you?"

Sage turned around to face him.

"Who the hell do you think you are?"

Roark closed on her, pressing his hand against her breastbone, gently but firmly forcing her into the corner with her back against the wall, his fingers wrapping around the back of her neck as his thumb caressed her throat.

"Such a willful, wild kitten. Do you have any idea how much I'm going to enjoy taking you and teaching you to purr just for me? Mine will be the only cream you lick from your lips."

He watched her struggle to remain standing, much less find words to respond in her normally cheeky manner as her breathing became shallow and erratic. He glanced down between them—her nipples were as hard as diamonds, their pebbled texture begging to be suckled. Then there was the bulge in the front of his jeans that wasn't getting any smaller. He'd wanted her from the moment he became sentient. There was no way of knowing if or when he'd be relegated back to the pages of her books, but he was beginning to believe he had escaped for good.

Before she could find her voice, he whirled her

around so once again, she was facing the corner. He wrapped one arm around her waist, trailing his fingers from her belly button to the small bundle of nerves at the apex of her thighs, stopping when he found her engorged clit. Inhaling sharply, he caught the sweet fragrance of her arousal. His fingers danced through the soft, silky, damp curls surrounding the tender bud, rolling it between finger and thumb. He might have to rethink keeping her bare. He rather liked the feel of her most intimate hair.

Sage moaned and braced herself against the fireplace. He'd never heard a more seductive sound, even when she was pleasuring herself. It called to the deepest part of him, the place where desire met libido, colliding until all that was left was pure lust. Thank God she hadn't written him as a pasty-faced pantywaist, who was all about political correctness and getting a permission form signed in triplicate before proceeding to the next stage of intimacy.

He'd never wanted any woman the way he wanted Sage. Everything about her called to him. Couldn't she see she needed him, not a one-night stand with no prayer of going anywhere? What she needed was what he wanted to be to her—partner, lover, and the one she answered to—in short, a Dom. She had written him with a strong, healthy sex drive and an overly endowed package to see to her needs. He had watched her pleasure herself often and had managed to seek her out in her dreams to satisfy her, but he knew that would pale in comparison to the pleasures of the real flesh he intended to indulge in.

He longed to have her naked, either on her knees or her belly—nothing but submissive sexual positions for his wild, feral kitten. He might occasionally allow her to be fucked on her back, but only if she'd been a very good girl. She needed to know who was in charge in all things—sexual and other. His cock had been straining against his fly since he'd picked her up off the ground by the Thames. None of the women she'd written for him had been anything other than a quick, hard fuck, but Sage was something altogether different. He wanted her in a way he had wanted no other. His cock throbbed all along his length, sending pulses down to his rock-hard balls—balls he meant to empty into her wet heat.

∼

Wildfire followed his fingers as they trailed down her body through the neat patch covering her mons. The instant he touched her clit, it felt as though fireworks were released within her system, feeling the heat and seeing their colors dancing before her eyes. He circled her clit, teasing, then brought his hand back to give it a hard pinch. She gasped, not sure if she felt pleasure or pain.

The knuckles of his other hand rasped against her backside as he unbuttoned his jeans.

Who wore button-fly jeans in the twenty-first century? No one she knew. No, whispered a little voice. Not no one… Roark—but he was a character in her book. This guy looked exactly like she had always seen him in her head and had described him, and he acted like Roark, except for the whole Dom thing—but that wasn't possible. Roark was someone she had created… a figment of her imagination. Or was he? the voice whispered again. Shut up! No one knew Roark was actually every hope, every dream, every fantasy she'd ever had rolled into one.

Not true. Like yourself, you hide Roark's true nature behind a strong, arrogant façade, but in your heart of hearts, you know the truth. You long for a man who will take you in hand, bend you to his will, yet cherish your heart and want to take care of you.

But no one knows, she argued with the voice.

He does, it said, drifting away.

Feeling him open his fly, freeing his cock and nudging it between her painful butt cheeks, she caught her breath and bit her lip. He shifted his hips, slipping his enormous cock between her legs, angling it toward the opening of her core. She tried clenching her thighs, but his sharp slap to her backside surprised her and she widened her stance. The smooth, uncut head of his cock slid along her soaked slit until he found her entrance.

"You're going to come when I mount you, aren't you? Do you understand me, Sage?" he said in a voice part growl, part purr, and completely seductive.

Sage could do nothing more than nod, moan, and lean more heavily against the wall as she felt him poised and ready to strike. His cock slid along the petals of her sex, gliding into the wetness he bared when he spread her labia. She groaned when she felt that first nudge that lodged him against her heated core. Shuddering, her entire body focused on what was about to occur—something that shouldn't happen, that couldn't be happening… yet it was.

Every nerve ending, every synapse, fired at an accelerated rate, and she worried the flames of desire would consume her, but she didn't care. She was strung as tightly as a bow ready to fire an arrow. His cock was targeted at her molten hub. She wanted him to surge forward, to impale her on his shaft. She needed him to fuck her. Didn't he understand that? Couldn't he sense it?

He swatted her again.

"I asked if you understood me."

She nodded. Another painful strike to her backside. She inhaled deeply, trying to keep from crying. God, she needed him—she needed him to fuck her. Why didn't he know that?

"Answer me, Sage," he said, tugging her clit and rubbing the end of his cock all around her slick labia.

"I understand," she mewled, hating the sound of her own voice.

"Better. Now say 'My Master is going to make me come when he mounts me.'"

Before he could spank her again, she said in a rush, the words tumbling out in a jumble, "My Master is going to make me come when he mounts me."

Sage found it difficult to believe he could achieve the result he wanted but wasn't in a position to argue the point. Besides, she was still having trouble processing everything that was taking place. She no longer doubted that he could make her respond in any way he wanted. It was better than any scene she'd ever written.

Without another word, Roark—she now knew, inexplicably, it was him—drove into her, surging forward in a single, powerful thrust that filled her to capacity and beyond. His length and girth stretched her in a way she'd never known before. She hadn't believed it was possible to orgasm just from the act of being mounted and possessed by a dominant man. Sage screamed and collapsed against the mantle, barely able to stand.

Roark stroked so deep and hard, every inch of her sheath felt his commanding presence as he hammered her pussy and ravaged her inner walls. She felt torn apart by his mounting and her resulting orgasm. He tightened his hold, and instinctively, she knew it wasn't to help her. He wanted to hold her in place while he fucked her. The pressure from his shaft pummeling her was overwhelming, and she climaxed again.

Sage tried to catch her breath to re-establish her equilibrium, but he wouldn't have it. He was in complete control, and she knew he was making that point. She barely had time to recover from her second orgasm before he ramped up his plunging and pushed her toward the abyss of a third. He fucked her relentlessly through another climax, never once slowing or changing the tempo—an unrelenting pounding that robbed her of her breath, her will, her ability to be anything other than what he demanded she be.

The speed and ferocity with which she responded to him were far beyond anything she had ever written, much less experienced in real life. She focused on the feel of his cock scraping her interior walls. She could not feel any twitching or thickening of his shaft, telltale signs he might be nearing his own release. There was only his ruthless stroking of her to ecstasy again and again. She tried to deny him, tried to withhold that last small inkling of herself, but he would have none of it.

Roark swatted her again along the top and sides of her bottom, making her cry out, wailing in both rapture and distress as she came not only from the driving force of his cock, but from the harsh strikes of his hand.

"Rule five… are we up to five? Doesn't matter. The next rule is you never withhold your responses, be it when I fuck you or crying when you're being spanked or welted. Your responses belong to me, and you will not try to keep them from me. Try it again, ever, and I will make you regret the day you created me." He punctuated each word with a hard surge forward or a stinging blow to her backside. Sage came repeatedly, shuddering in his arms again and again as he took what they both knew to be his.

"One more time, kitten," he crooned in her ear. "Come for me and milk my cock dry."

He redoubled his efforts, riding her with a surety bordering on arrogance. She was certain she had nothing left to give him, but knew he would have what he wanted. The fact he could so completely undo her the first time they were together was frightening. Roark demanded her response as easily as her obedience. Nothing she'd ever experienced—either in real life or in prose—

had prepared her for the sexual dominance he inflicted on her.

Sage's wails became moans, then morphed into whimpers when the next orgasm bore down on her. Thankfully, she felt his impending release. She cried out one last time and collapsed in his arms as he spurted what felt like great ropes of cum into her wrecked sheath, bathing it with his creamy essence as though it could soothe the fire raging within her. With a last brutal thrust, Roark forced her over the edge into a void where time and space no longer existed—only this man and being used by him. Her pussy clamped down, contracting all along his length, milking every last gush of his semen and pulling it deep inside her. His release seemed endless, and Sage could do nothing but endure as he held her in place.

When at last it was over, Roark swung her up in his arms and carried her back to the bed, drawing back the covers and laying her down on the side furthest from the door.

"I'd like to freshen up," she said quietly as he sat on the edge of the bed, pulling off his boots and socks. Then she registered the fact that while she had been naked, Roark had been fully clothed with only his fly open, so his cock was free to fuck her.

"Why? You won't stay that way for long. I've waited a long time for you, Sage. I don't believe there's a way for me to be pulled back, but I'm not taking any chances. For however long I'm here, I mean to make the most of it and of you. If I'm still here in the morning, we'll try to figure out who tried to have you killed. If I'm not, you call Holmes at Scotland Yard and do exactly what he tells you."

"I'm not sure my need to fuck you is enough to keep me free from the pages of your books," he continued, "but I suspect keeping you alive is. In any event, I won't go back without one hell of a fight, but if I get sucked back in, and you disobey me or put yourself in danger, I'll find my way back to the physical world, and the first thing I'll do is welt your ass then fuck it. Trust me, Sage, you don't want your first ass fucking from your Master to be when he's pissed and looking to teach you a lesson."

"So, you *are* Roark?" she whispered.

"Who the bloody hell else would I be?" he answered, mildly annoyed and standing up to finish undressing.

He crossed over to the bed, unashamedly naked. She rolled to the opposite side of the bed, watching him and wincing as her bottom briefly made contact with the mattress. Why the hell shouldn't he be? She'd described him more than once as a sexy beast, and he was. He unfastened his vintage Rolex, placing it on the dresser with his wallet before returning and placing his gun on the nightstand furthest from the window.

"Shove over, Sage. You know I always sleep closest to the door."

Sage scooched over, careful to avoid her butt making contact with the bed again, then didn't move. She had to be dreaming, or whoever tried to kill her had given her the worst—or best—acid trip ever.

Like he always did in her books, Roark rolled her away from him, chuckling when she gasped from the brief contact of ass to mattress. He wrapped his arm around her waist and pulled her back to snuggle against him, his cock nestled in the cleft of her buttocks, his hand resting possessively on her mons. She tried squirming away to get a little distance between them, but he just pinched her clit and kept applying pressure until she wriggled back where he wanted her.

"You stay where I put you, Sage. Next time, you'll earn yourself more than just a pinch."

All that had happened in the past twelve hours or so came crashing down on her, and Sage quietly started crying. In a move she'd never written for him, he stroked her gently and kissed her neck, nuzzling her nape under her hair.

"It's all right, love. No one will ever harm you again. That's not to say you won't get spanked or that I won't cause you a bit of pain when warranted, but you're safe with me. Your safe word is 'hero.'"

"You might have mentioned that before now."

"Why? Would you have used it?"

"No…"

Was she safe with him? What if she wasn't? Or what if she was, but he disappeared into the pages of her book, never to return?

CHAPTER 9

He gave Sage little sleep—he couldn't seem to help himself. He slept restlessly, and every time he woke, he reached for her, finding his libido every bit as strong, if not stronger, than she had portrayed in her books. More than once, he pulled her to him, bringing her under him to mount and use with long, hard strokes. He knew she had to be sore but found he didn't care. He needed her, and she needed him. He needed to bind her to him in every way he could. Even after he'd exhausted her, she never failed to provide him with the response he wanted. Sage seemed surprised at the depth of her carnal nature and her ability to experience multiple orgasms. Each time he rode her, she responded quicker and more intensely, allowing him to revel in her ability to provide him with such pleasure.

He woke, his cock poking at her backside. Never had she written a woman who could compare to her—quick to respond, wildly passionate, and infinitely satisfying. Each time he felt her sheath contract around his shaft, it was as if it had always been this way. Memories of the others she had forced him to endure faded away with each encounter.

Rolling her onto her belly, he knelt behind her and grasped her hips, pulling her up into position—ass up, upper torso and head down. He grinned when he reached between her legs to stroke her silky slit. He had yet to not find her wet and waiting. He guided his staff to the entrance of her core, pushing forward before she was fully awake. She groaned as a small orgasm rippled through her body. He stroked her hard and fast until she came screaming into the pillow as he thrust home and spent his seed deep inside her. Releasing her, he tipped her back over onto her side, settling back into his normal place, and pulled her close. He smiled when she didn't try to wriggle away.

"Tell me something… why is it in the books, you always have your women on top, sliding up and down your cock while you play with their tits and clit, but you have yet to fuck me face-to-face?"

He barked a laugh, idly fondling her nipples.

"Naughty girls only get fucked on their back as a treat when they've been very good, but are never allowed on top. You, my love, will almost always be fucked in very submissive positions to remind you I am the one in charge, not you. To that end, and to get a handle on your behavior, I've decided to put you on maintenance spankings twice a week."

"Twice a week?" she squeaked. "That doesn't seem fair."

"Fair is whatever I define it to be. We'll start with twice a week and see how it goes. You behave yourself, and I may adjust it down. You decide to challenge my authority and misbehave, I'll increase it to three times a week or more. You will not be allowed to continue down this self-destructive path you seem determined to travel. You're going to follow the rules I give you, and when you don't, you will be punished."

He slipped his hand between them and gently massaged her dark rosebud. She tried to shift away from his invasive finger, but he pinched her nipple until she submitted and didn't try to evade his touch.

"In case you missed it, love, the power dynamic between us has shifted. You are no longer in control of anything. You belong to me… all of you. You exist to please me in the same way I exist to pleasure and keep you safe. That means your body belongs to me—all of it. You don't abuse it. You're going to start eating right…"

"I eat fine," she said with a pout she didn't know she was capable of.

"Chips and caramel corn are not proper nutrition. And here's a big one, you do not seek to pleasure yourself unless I tell you to. I tossed the vibrator you brought here into the rubbish last night. I will see to all your sexual needs."

"You expect me to agree to this?"

"Did I ask for your agreement?" He chuckled. "Be a good girl and tell me you're going to follow the rules. Tell me that when you don't, you expect me to discipline you in whatever way I deem best."

Sage said nothing. He'd enveloped her in a sensual haze, combining soft caresses with his silky voice. She melted back into his body, answering his call and agreeing to everything, but he needed her to say it. The fingers that rolled and gently squeezed her nipples pinched them hard until her body stiffened and she yelped.

"Did you hear me, Sage? I need to know you understand."

"I do," she said, sighing with a combination of arousal and resignation, and snuggled back into his body, instinctively seeking his strength and comfort.

"Then you say it. Tell me you know you belong to me, that you understand and expect when you misbehave that I will curb your errant behavior. Tell me you're going to be a good girl and try to follow the rules."

"Yes, Sir," she said, trying out the honorarium for the first time.

"All of it, Sage."

Taking a deep breath, she said, "I belong to you, Sir. If you decide I've been bad…"

"You are never bad, love. You just misbehave sometimes. Try again."

"I belong to you." *Why was there so much comfort and joy in saying those four little words?* "I will try to follow your rules. If I don't or misbehave, you will punish me."

"That's my good girl," he murmured seductively. Rubbing her backside lightly, he chuckled when she winced from the lightest contact. "You have a beautifully responsive bottom, Sage. It colors easily and well and has the most delightful give and bounce when my hand lands."

"I'm so glad you enjoy it," she said with a touch of snark.

"Careful, Sage. Start sassing me and I'll drag you out of this bed, wash your mouth out with soap, then spank you until you're crying and begging me to stop. For the record, if you earn yourself a discipline spanking when you're already scheduled for maintenance, you'll receive the discipline spanking, and maintenance will be moved to the next day."

"How did you learn all this? I didn't write you like this."

"But you wanted to," he whispered. "You created me for yourself. You never told anyone what you wanted and instinctively knew you needed, but I knew. Go to sleep, Sage."

He felt her sag against him as sleep claimed her. Once she rested peacefully, he kissed her cheek and sat up on the edge of the bed. Sage fidgeted; he leaned over to kiss her again and stroked her body until she settled.

Who tried to kill her… and why? Did any of the incidents in North Carolina have anything to do with this latest attempt on her life? Were they part and parcel of the same thing?

Roark got up and pulled on his jeans, then grabbed her laptop and stretched back out on the bed. He worked his way through, looking for information on the net while not being a part of it. He idly wondered if he could move back and forth between the two existences, but was unwilling to try, fearing if he succeeded in returning to the ether of her laptop, he might never escape it again. Sage needed him here in the physical world. She needed him to protect her from this clear-and-present danger, as well as from herself.

Running his hand down her body and rubbing her still slightly colored backside, he smiled at her preening under his attention.

"Don't worry, Sage. I'm here, and I'm going to take good care of you."

He watched the news and learned the body of the man who tried to kill Sage had been found and identified as a killer for hire. So, no motive for the man himself, but somebody hired him. Sage didn't seem to know anything, and nothing he knew led him to believe she'd done anything that would warrant notice from any criminal element, much less something of the magnitude they'd want her dead. No one knew her better than he did, including Sage herself. She wrote erotic romance books, for God's sake, not in-depth investigative journalism pieces, exposing the wrongdoings of someone in power.

Roark pulled up her financial documents and began combing them. At first glance, they appeared to be in order, but something kept tickling his brain—something was off, something didn't seem quite right. He ordered room service and leaned over to nuzzle and kiss her awake.

She opened her eyes and seemed confused at first.

"Roark?"

"Yes, love, I'm here. I've ordered breakfast. Why don't you go hop in the shower?"

"The hotel knows you're here?"

"It's where I live. I had the butler bring up the ice last night."

"You… you don't really exist," she whispered.

He patted her backside, smiling when she

winced. "Your bottom seems to think I exist, and I am rather sure your pussy is well aware of it. Maybe I should reinsert the butt plug, so you have a constant reminder that I'm here and now in the physical world."

"No, that won't be necessary. Did they seemed surprised at all that you were calling?"

"Not at all. As far as anyone can tell, you, Felix, Holmes, and I are the only ones who are aware that until recently, the three of us only existed in the pages of your books."

She nodded. "The weird thing is that the names in the books have all been changed, and all of you are sentient… and solid. I mean, it's not like you're an apparition I can put my hands through."

"And aren't you glad my cock is nice and solid," he teased, kissing her when she smiled. "In some ways, it feels a bit odd, but in others, it feels as if I've always been here. I don't want you to worry about that. I will ensure that you are safe, which leads me to another rule."

"Pfft… you and your ru—"

Her statement was cut off when he flipped her on her belly and his hand connected with her backside in a hard swat.

"My rules, Sage, are to be followed. Deviation from the rules gets you spanked or more. Now, as I was saying before you interrupted me… Until further notice, you do not leave this room or open the door without my permission. Understood?"

Sage nodded but didn't say anything.

Another harsh smack.

"You answer with words when I ask you a question. Do you understand?"

"Yes," she said sullenly.

He landed another painful swat to her ass.

"Yes, what?" he barked. "Watch the attitude, Sage. If you need a spanking in order to behave, you let me know. Do you?"

"No, Sir, I don't need a spanking, and yes, Sir, I understand."

He hid his grin when she backed off.

"Better," he said, idly petting her bottom. "Aren't you supposed to be taking a shower?"

"I don't remember you being so bossy."

"And I don't remember you being so sassy. When you get showered, we'll have breakfast and lay out the rest of the day."

~

Sage stood under the shower, letting the hot, steamy water pelt down on her. The shower in Roark's suite was nothing like the one she'd had previously. For one thing, it was larger and had all the high-tech, pulsating jets anyone could ever want. She didn't know the Savoy offered this kind of bathroom, but she'd written it into a book.

A book? How the hell could this be happening? Was this all some crazy dream? Had she died? If so, was this heaven or hell? Maybe she was just in a coma and would wake—but what if she didn't want to?

Regardless, it seemed she had no choice but to keep moving forward. Stepping out of the shower, she was drying herself when she heard the sound of breakfast being delivered. She donned what she assumed was Roark's cashmere robe—it, too, was exactly as she described in the books and hadn't been in the bath the day before. She wandered back into the living room suite.

"Thank you, Mr. Samuels," said the waiter. "Is there anything you and Ms. Matthews need? Shall I have them bring up additional towels?"

Sage watched Roark peel off several large denomination bills.

"That would be very thoughtful. If you could also ask them to replace at least half of my love's Diet Coke with water, that would be beneficial. She's apparently forgotten she isn't allowed to drink as many of those as she has been of late."

"Is there anything else I can bring to make Ms. Matthews more comfortable?"

"Uhm, I'm right here. You might ask me if I need anything," Sage said testily.

Roark turned and scowled. It was all she could

do not to shrink back, but she could feel her butt clenching.

"Sage, apologize. The staff is trying to see to your comfort and do not deserve the sharp side of your writer's tongue."

He stared her down until she dropped her eyes and mumbled, "I apologize. Roark is right. Thank you for your consideration."

"That's my good girl," he purred. "No, Ms. Matthews will be fine with me, provided she drops the attitude and behaves herself."

Just as Roark was closing the door, there was a light tap, and he admitted Felix into the room.

He looked around conspiratorially and lowered his voice, "Are we expecting trouble, sir?"

"I don't mean to be rude, Felix, but Roark's told me you and DSI Holmes are aware that until recently, you only existed in the pages of my books. Can I ask you something?"

"Of course, you can, Sage, anything at all," Felix said kindly.

"Do you know you don't look at all like I described you in the book?"

He chuckled. "Yes, and I am grateful for that. Poor Holmes still got stuck with the name you gave him."

"It was supposed to just be a joke for readers."

"Yes, love, but unfortunately, the DSI is the butt of your joke. You have a bad habit of giving characters, except for your hero here and his ever-changing bevy of beauties, truly terrible names."

Sage felt heat creep up her cheeks. "Uhm, sorry about that. I guess it never occurred to me that it would matter to any of you. I'll apologize to Holmes the next time I see him. And if you don't like Felix, how about Spense… you know for your last name."

"Spense," he said, nodding. "Yes. I think I rather fancy that."

Suddenly curious, she asked, "Are all the characters in the books sentient?"

"Not all. The only one you haven't met is Eddy…"

Sage brightened. "Edouard? The hacker? He exists? Is he here?"

"No, he's still inside the book, but we can communicate with him," Felix answered. "You captured his personality completely. He doesn't want to come out."

"As for trouble, I rather imagine it's already here, despite Sage's inability to do as she's told to keep herself safe."

Felix chuckled. "I rather suspect now that you're here, that will change." He dropped his voice back to a whisper, "You wouldn't know anything about that killer they found, would you?"

"He was trying to kill Sage," Roark said dismissively. "I've called Holmes and let him know."

"Thus, why they found the body. I take it Sage will remain here with you?" Felix looked over at her. "You couldn't be in safer hands, you know."

"Yes, I know," she said. It still fascinated her that she was actually talking to one of her characters. *This must be a dream or a coma.* Any minute she expected the theme from the *Twilight Zone* to start playing.

"Did you know Roark would be able to get out when you moved me to the suite I described as his?" she asked.

"I knew he was planning to try. It was curious to both Holmes and me that we found ourselves here, yet something was blocking Roark's escape."

"And yes, Felix, Sage will be here with me from now on."

"Yes, Sir. I'll see that the hotel extends her every courtesy," Felix offered before leaving the room.

Roark removed the cloches. "Eggs benedict, bagels and lox, strawberry blintzes, broiled grapefruit, scalloped potatoes, and bacon… lots and lots of bacon."

She grinned. "If I'm not careful, between you and Felix, I'm going to be the size of a blimp. I didn't see a lot of that on any of the menus."

"They only prepare this kind of specialized thing for special guests… just like in The Corpse Stalked the Dawn."

"I need to wake up. Seriously, this is weird," she muttered to herself.

"What you need, my love, is to sit down and have something to eat."

"I'm not really hungry… and I'd prefer to limit having to sit down this morning."

Roark chuckled. "You may use a couple of pillows, but you will eat either sitting on the pillows or impaled on my cock."

She felt the blood drain from her face, knowing that he wasn't making a joke or an idle threat.

"So, you know something about the man who tried to kill me?" she asked, crossing the room and grabbing an extra pillow to sit on while at the dining table.

"Not much. He was an assassin for hire, but not a particularly good one. Think! Have you written something in a book I don't know about? Have you crossed anyone? Any threatening mail?" he said, joining her at the table so they could share their first meal.

"No. Honestly, Roark, I have no idea why that guy tried to kill me."

"What about the threatening letters? The shots fired at you? The hanging body? You don't think that's important to consider?" Roark said, annoyed.

"How do you know about those?"

"Anything that came across your computer before I got out, I've seen."

"Couldn't he just be a random sociopath looking to get his rocks off?" she asked hopefully.

"The man wasn't a sociopath. He was a hired killer who wouldn't go after you without being paid. So, we need to find out who wants you dead."

"I hope that scowl isn't directed at me," she said quietly.

He chuckled. Sage was falling in love with the sound of his voice as well as his touch, his arrogance, and his protective nature. *The fact was, she was fast losing her heart to her own creation. Was he right? Had she created him to fulfill her own fantasies?*

"Not unless you played with yourself in the shower."

She leaned across the table. "No, I was my Master's good girl."

"The scowl is because when I was in the book, I could directly connect with other systems. I'm going to go back through your emails and financials. Now I have to either use your laptop or print them out."

"What do you mean, back through?"

He stood up and kissed the top of her head. "Love, there isn't much about your life I don't already know. If it's ever been electronic, I've seen it. Besides, keeping secrets from me will get you spanked so fast, it'll spin your head around."

She laughed. "I have written so many scenes where you said that to heroines, and the mere words made butterflies go off in their bellies. I never thought it was true. I mean, I've read the literature, and I've been to a couple of clubs, but…"

"You, my sweet girl, have always wanted to be submissive."

"No," she said, shaking her head, "I haven't. I've always been a feminist, never wanted to answer to anyone."

"That's what you tell the world, but when you pleasure yourself, you long for a dominant man to take charge, to watch over you, to care for you, to demand the best of you, to enforce his will over yours…"

"No," she whispered, frightened it might be true.

"Then why, oh why did you write me to fulfill every fantasy you've ever had? It's all right, Sage. I'm here now."

"But what happens if you disappear just as quickly?" she asked, acknowledging her true fear.

"That won't happen," he said with confidence backed by a will of iron. "And if it did, I would move heaven and earth to return to you in the flesh. I've been with you many times. I've spent more than one night between your legs, having you to my heart's content."

"No… you mean those dreams…"

"Were the mere remnants of the time we spent together. I was as much a captive of my fate as you. I had planned to try to come through last night when I knew the veils between the two worlds would be at its thinnest. So, when your life was in peril, the need to protect and save you from your own foolishness gave me the strength to break free. Now that I have had a taste of the reality that is you, can you not imagine what I would do to remain with you? To revel in the exquisite carnal and other pleasures I find in your arms and between your thighs? As I was able to do so before, believe me when I tell you… nothing will keep me from your side."

"Promise?" she said in a small voice filled with longing and need.

He smiled. "I do indeed, and neither the badass Roark nor your Dom will ever break their promise. While I'm reviewing things, why don't you start your next novel?"

"What do I write? I mean, you, at least as Roark, don't exist anymore, and I don't know if I'm going to like the guy who replaced you. Even if I could write you, I don't think I could write you with other women," she said, knowing she was babbling.

"That makes me happy to hear that. I like your idea about the wolf shifters who have packs with vineyards all along the Pacific Coast of the States. Why don't you write that?"

He made himself comfortable at the desk, spreading out a great many papers to study while Sage set herself up with her laptop.

Roark poured over all the financial data available. He looked over to see Sage frantically pounding the keyboard in a way she hadn't done in years.

"Having fun, love?"

She looked up, grinning. "Yes. My readers are going to love this."

"I'm going down to chat with Felix. I'd like to get Eddy working on this and see if he knows a more efficient way to go over all this financial data."

"Do you think there's something wrong with it?"

"Yes, but I can't tell you why. It just seems off. I'm not a finance man for the most part, but I keep thinking I should be able to make the numbers add up… and they don't. I'm hoping Eddy or the Yard's forensic accounting unit can get a better handle on them. I'd also like a word with Gabriel Watson."

Sage smiled. "Jealous?"

"Not really. I know how you feel about me, but I also know you were very attracted to Watson. I just want to thank him for his help and ensure he knows you are most definitely not available." He started toward the door and then stopped and turned back. "Sage?"

"Yes?"

"How acrimonious was your split from Gail Vincent?"

"She wasn't happy, but she wouldn't let me write anything but you."

"Was that the only reason you left?"

"Mostly. Why do you ask?" she said, closing the laptop and swiveling in the chair.

"It comes back to the financials. As I say, I can't really put my finger on it, but it doesn't seem to add up the way I think it should."

"You know, I asked her about that once and she told me the formulas were too complicated."

"Nothing about financials should be complicated unless it's set up that way to deliberately confuse and deceive someone looking at them. Go back to work, take a nap, or watch television. I'll be back in a bit."

"Ok," she said absently and turned back to her laptop. "I might pop downstairs to the third floor for a swim."

"Really? And how would you expect to do that without opening the door to our suite or leaving the room?"

"Seriously? Come on, Roark, it's the Savoy, for heaven's sake. What could happen?"

Roark walked back to her and leaned against the table.

"I knew that when I made the rule. Break the rule, Sage, and I can assure you won't like the consequences." He chuckled. "That's not completely true. You won't like part of your punishment, and you really won't like that you like the rest. Keep in mind what I said about my taking your ass for the first time with you sporting a set of welts when I'm pissed. Don't do it."

Kissing the top of her head and leaving her in their room, Roark walked briskly down the hall and took the lift down to the main floor. He asked the front desk to find Felix since he wasn't at his usual post. He was still a bit surprised when the staff seemed to know people who, until the last few nights, had only existed on the pages of Sage's books. Before Felix could be located, Gabriel Watson approached him.

"Roark, I'm glad you're back."

"As am I. I wanted to personally thank you for your assistance in keeping Sage safe."

The tall blond chuckled. "Not as well as I would have liked. She's not very good at following directions, is she?"

Roark smiled. "She has her moments. For the most part, she minds me, but then I provide her with the structure and support she needs."

"I understand. I must say when I first met her, I was unaware you had given up your womanizing ways or that Sage was attached to you."

"I have, and she is," Roark said in a steely tone. "When a man finds a rare woman of Sage's fire and passion, he would be a fool not to do everything in his power to make her his."

"Yes, Holmes said something very similar. But should she ever seek shelter elsewhere…"

"She won't."

"Mr. Samuels," Felix hailed from across the lobby. "How may I be of assistance?"

Roark faced off with the Head of Security, each man taking the measure of the other as Felix joined them.

"Well, I'm sure Sage is safe with you. Should you need my assistance, please let me know," Watson said.

Roark inclined his head as Gabe turned back toward his office.

"Felix, what were you thinking, allowing that man to get close to Sage," he snarled.

"I didn't know if you'd be able to pierce the veil, and I wanted her safe."

"Of course, forgive me. I find I'm a bit more overly protective of Sage than I had counted on. Let's you and I go for a walk."

"Do you think we can leave the hotel? I told them my flat was being painted, so I've been staying here. I'm a bit concerned about being away from whatever may be anchoring us to this place."

"I don't think it's an issue. I was down by the Thames, and Holmes has been going between here, the Yard, and his home."

"Odd feeling, isn't it?" Felix dropped his voice.

"Knowing until just recently, we only existed on the pages of Sage's books?"

"What I'm finding fascinating is everyone seems to know us."

"I agree," Felix said, smiling as they walked outside. "How can I help?"

"As you know, someone tried to have killed Sage last night. I need to figure out who. Trying to access the dark web from out here is a lot more difficult than when I was inside and connected."

"Eddy should be able to help."

"So, you can communicate with him as well and vice versa?"

"Yes. He managed to stay in the book, but I've been able to reach out. What is it you need, Roark?"

"Everything he can find on an American publisher, Gail Vincent, and the hired killer."

"Do you think your need to protect her allowed all of us to leave her books?"

"Probably. It's strange, though, isn't it?"

Felix smiled. "Very. I'll see what Eddy can find."

CHAPTER 10

*R*oark headed back to their room, smiling at how quickly he had accepted not only his new reality, but sharing his life and everything in it with Sage. He wondered if she had any idea of the depth of his feelings for her. Since she no longer wrote his dialogue, he hoped he would be able to find the words. Thinking of her waiting for him made his cock stiffen. If she wanted to go swimming, he'd take her down tonight after the pool was closed, and they'd go skinny dipping. She could be his personal mermaid. Between now and then, he meant to take her back to bed and have at her. God, he was like a randy schoolboy.

Stepping into the lift, he looked at the buttons. Their suite was on the sixth floor, but he feared if he went all the way up, he would find the room empty. Hoping against hope, he pushed the button for the third floor. He knew her sometimes better than she knew herself. He entered the atrium that housed the pool. It was empty save for a lone swimmer. He stealthily approached the end of the pool she was swimming toward.

When she reached the end of the pool, Roark grasped the top of her head so she couldn't see who it was or break the surface. He pushed down, preventing her from coming up for air or swimming away. Sage's hands flailed. He could almost feel her panic and desperation as she tried to break free. He held her under the water long enough to scare her, but not long enough to hurt her. When he released her head, he grabbed her by the ponytail she had used to pull her hair back and hauled her above the surface of the water.

Waiting until she saw it was him and she had placed her feet on the bottom of the pool, he silently dragged her toward the steps and helped her out. He handed her a towel and started back toward their room without releasing his hold or saying a word. The minute the door to their suite latched behind them, he let go and propelled her toward the bed.

"I can explain," she started.

"So can I. You thought you'd just do what you wanted with no thought to your safety or the rules. The first isn't unexpected, but I'd thought I'd made more of an impression on you. I will correct that and ensure you understand the depth of my displeasure with your behavior. Strip."

"Roark..."

"Strip, Sage. Now," he commanded.

He watched the struggle play across her features. She was at war with herself. He knew part of her desperately wanted to submit, but it battled with the part of her that had convinced herself that it was wrong to do so.

He battled as well. He would have preferred for this early time together to be more about whispered words, promises, and assurances that everything would be fine and that he would keep her safe. Unfortunately, his woman was proving to be tenacious and unruly. She needed to learn to follow the rules, regardless of whether she *wanted* to or not.

"You broke the rules and put yourself in danger, didn't you?"

"It's a stupid rule. I'm perfectly safe here at the Savoy."

"Are you forgetting someone hired a professional killer to end your life? Do you think he wouldn't have killed you here at the Savoy if you'd brought him back to your bed?"

"No, I didn't forget, and I didn't bring him back here to fuck," she said heatedly.

"No, you were quite prepared to let him fuck you under a bridge."

That silenced her.

"That's really not relevant to this discussion," she said.

"You're right. The only salient point to our discussion is you disobeyed me, knowing full well what the consequences would be, didn't you?"

"Well, yes, but I just wanted to swim."

"No, that isn't it at all. What you wanted was to see if you could disobey me and not have me punish you. Guess what, love? I would never disappoint you. Avoiding a punishment when you have willfully disobeyed me is not going to happen. More to the point, you don't want it to, do you?"

Tears began to well in her eyes, and she shook her head.

Roark softened his demeanor as he took a seat on the edge of the bed.

"That's my good girl," he crooned. "Take off your bathing suit and put yourself in position over my knee. You know I'm going to spank you, don't you?"

She nodded, removing her suit and revealing her aroused body, then started toward him. She halted, her eyes pleading, but he wasn't sure for what and doubted she knew, either. He patted his hard thigh and waited for her to accept what she already knew in her soul to be true. With a stifled sob, she assumed the position every female with a dominant partner had been taking since the dawn of time.

Roark was so proud of her. He knew what those few steps had cost her—his proud, defiant woman had made the decision to submit to him and trusted he would safeguard her heart. He meant to humble her but planned to tell her later that at that moment, he felt humbled, too, that giving herself to him was everything.

He raised his hand and brought it down sharply, beginning a flurry of hard swats across her upturned rump, first one side, then the other. With harsh slaps he spanked her, encompassing her entire bottom, overlapping them so their distinctiveness disappeared, and her bottom turned from ivory to pink to red.

Sage squirmed, trying to get away, but he clamped his leg across the backs of hers so her efforts failed. He didn't hold it against her since he understood it was all part of the ritual. She would resist, especially as the pain intensified, but he would never consider stopping until she completely capitulated to his dominance.

Over and over he spanked her, focusing at first on the fullest part of her bottom, staining it a dark red. Every so often, he changed it up and landed a few targeted blows to the juncture of her ass and the top of her thighs.

The longer and harder he punished her, the more

engorged his cock became. The bulge in the front of his jeans had been growing since he'd first entered the elevator and had become painful as he fished her out of the pool. What he really wanted was to stop, toss her over the end of the bed, step up between her legs, and hammer her pussy until she was raw and sore, but right now, her need to be disciplined superseded his need to dominate her in an entirely different manner.

In order to focus on her needs before seeing to his own, Roark redoubled the strength and fury of his swats, causing her to yowl in response. He meant to ensure while she might find walking difficult immediately after he finished fucking her, she would feel the after-effects of this spanking for the next several days. He meant to bring home the lesson each time he slammed his hips into her bruised and swollen backside as he thrust forward, ramming his cock to the end of her sheath.

Roark wanted her to be as aroused as he was when he let her up, so he began splaying his hand and deliberately catching the tender spot between her legs. Her sharp inhalation of breath let him know he'd found his target. He wanted her sore… and soaked. Every time he struck her labia, his fingers came back bearing the evidence of her arousal. Sage's sobs of pain began to be overshadowed by moans of pleasure.

He rested his hand on the inside of her thigh

and reached forward to tickle her swollen nub, letting her writhe. Trailing his fingers along the lips of her wet, swollen labia, he stroked and parted them to tease the entrance to her sheath, a gaping opening begging to be filled. He landed several open-handed swats squarely between her legs, making her wail in distress and need.

"Roark, stop. I shouldn't have done it. I won't do it again!"

"If the killer had found you alone in that pool, you'd be dead. You're going to learn to mind me and follow the rules."

∽

Thank God he stopped. I almost came when he was spanking me.

She took deep lungfuls of air and began to breathe a bit more easily when he released the vice grip of his legs trapping hers. Helping her to her feet, he fisted her hair and led her to the corner. It wasn't unexpected. What did catch her off guard was instead of moving away from her, he moved behind her, unbuttoned the fly of his jeans, and released his cock, throbbing in need. It was all she could do to stifle her own needy moan. If he needed to fuck her… she needed him to do it even more. She knew this was punishment sex, pure and simple, but her pussy pulsed in rhythm to his need all the same.

He ran his hands lightly up and down the side of her torso, alternating between fingertips and knuckles. Her body shuddered in anticipation and advanced arousal. Caressing her bottom with one hand, he guided the head of his hot staff to her wet sheath, pausing just outside her opening.

For the love of God, what was he waiting for? She pushed back to try to engage his cock. The crack across her backside was loud and harsh.

"Don't you dare forget yourself with me, Sage. I'm the one who does the mounting, not you. I want you to feel every single inch of my cock as I take possession of what belongs to me."

"Please, Roark, I want you…" she mewled in frustration and need.

"Oh, I know, love, but before I'm done, your pussy is going to be as sore and swollen as your backside. And after I've filled your pussy with my cream, I'm going to fill your bottom hole as well."

Slowly, Roark surged forward, inch by tantalizing inch, sinking deep inside her. Sage collapsed against the wall, her orgasm bursting forth to encompass them both with its power and simplicity. She needed nothing more than to be filled with him. Had Roark not held her hips, her knees would have buckled, and she'd have hit the floor.

"You need me to spank you hard and fuck you harder, don't you, Sage?"

Thrusting slowly, he exaggerated the motion that dragged his length along her inner walls, pushing to her depths and ensuring his hard pelvis bumped her tender behind, then dragged his cock back, almost retreating completely and surging forward again. This wasn't just punishment sex, not just dominance—this was Roark taking complete control and possession, offering no mercy and giving no quarter. Sage arched her back, offering deeper penetration along with her utter surrender.

"I'm going to fuck you until you learn to behave." He timed the rough pumping of his hips to punctuate each word.

His fingers dug into her tender flesh as he held her in place, thrusting with more vigor, his pelvis slamming into her punished ass, his cock hammering her pussy so she was in no doubt who was in control. Roark released the hold on one of her hips, his fist in her hair drawing her ear close to his mouth.

"I'm going to fuck your sore bottom when I'm done with your pussy. I'm going to fill it up and make you scream with need. What is it they say in the song? It's going to hurt so good. You want that, don't you, Sage?"

His onslaught showed no signs of slowing or of his impending release. She climaxed again, praying at some point, he'd empty himself in her. There was a part of her that thought about the wrongness of what he was doing, but nothing had ever felt more right. The greater part of her—the part that took flight and soared among the heavens where there was only light—had never felt sexier, safer, more submissive, and seductive all at the same time.

Roark knew her in a way no other being ever could or would. He knew exactly what to say and how to say it to invoke that secretly submissive woman who had laid dormant for so many years. She had never liked anal, but the thought of giving herself to him that way had an allure that was undeniable. Sage wanted to feel his staff stroking her back passage in the same way he did her sheath. She needed to feel that painful stretch of her puckered rosebud as he pressed forward, humbling her at the same time he set her free. She knew he meant to encourage her to embrace all that she was, not just the parts she thought were socially acceptable.

"Good girl," he crooned. "Come for me again."

Repeatedly, he plunged into her, plundering her pussy so it pulsed and trembled all along his length. She was getting just what she needed, a good hard ramming, and reveled in his embrace. Her vaginal walls trembled. She couldn't process the intensity of her own emotions, feelings he called forth so easily. Her breath quickened and became labored, her moans morphing into whimpers before only silence greeted her oncoming climax, and her legs stiffened in anticipation as he gave a last brutal thrust, releasing a torrent of cum into her depths.

Roark leaned against her, pressing her into the wall, trying to catch his breath. He uncoupled from her, nuzzling her neck and kissing her gently as the overflow from his seed dribbled down her thighs. Turning her around, he placed his hand on top of her head, and just as he had in the pool, he pressed down, forcing her to her knees.

Sage wrapped her hand around the length of his cock, fisting him gently as she wet her lips. Opening her mouth, she wasn't prepared when he cupped the back of her skull, held her in place, and drove his semi-erect cock deep into her mouth. She had to suppress her gag reflex as he pushed into the back of her throat.

"Get me nice and clean, but you'd better get me hard and well lubed before I pull it out."

Sage was good at giving head, always liked the feeling of power and control it gave her, but this… this was not her giving Roark a blow job. No, this was Roark fucking her mouth, using it before he took her bottom hole—the only one he hadn't had his cock in today. She was proud of her skills and was pleased with herself when he loosened his hold of her head and allowed her to service him. The idea that she was his fuck toy, and he'd use her however, whenever, wherever he wanted, spiked her arousal, and she wanted desperately to pinch her own nipples. She had never been with a man who wasn't circumcised and wondered why she had bestowed that detail on Roark. Her tongue traced every vein and fold of his cock as it grew rigid again, enjoying the difference of his staff from the others she had known. She hadn't expected him to recover so quickly.

He chuckled in a deeply satisfied and masculine way.

"My girl knows how to suck cock."

He helped her up off her knees, but she couldn't meet his eyes. Looking down, Sage could see both her saliva and his pre-cum dripping from the end of his cock. A part of her wanted to protest, to somehow withhold this last bastion of her power and pride, but she knew it would be an empty gesture. Her need to feel him possess her in this last intimate act of claiming was too great.

"Ask me to fuck your ass, Sage."

She said nothing but nodded.

"Not good enough. Say it!" he growled.

"Roark, please?" She begged, but wasn't sure what she was begging for. Was it for him to breach her bottom hole with his cock or not have to ask him to do it?

"Do you want me to stroke your bottom hole the way I do your pussy?" She nodded. "Do you need me to spend myself in your dark channel so it's filled with my cum? Is that what you want?"

"Yes," she said brokenly.

"Ask me."

Taking a deep breath, she opened her eyes as he tilted her face toward his and nodded to encourage her.

"Roark, will you please fuck my ass?"

"Yes, love. I will use your bottom hole for my pleasure… and yours." He smiled. "You're going to like this a lot more than you're going to want to. I promise."

He led her to the bed and helped her up on her hands and knees. Sliding his hand along her spine, from her rump to the nape of her neck, he pressed her down into the mattress while nudging her legs apart. Roark grasped her hips and pressed his cock against her tight, dark rosebud.

"You want me to fuck your pretty bottom hole?"

She could only nod. She had lost the ability and the will to respond verbally or deny her own need.

Roark positioned his cock and began to penetrate her, slowly but determinedly, inch-by-inch. His control was absolute as he pushed his staff past the tight ring of muscle. He didn't seem rushed; it was as if he planned to use all the time in the world to show her a new way to be pleasured and to ensure she enjoyed it. It might have been easier to take had he simply sought his own pleasure in a way that humbled her. But he hadn't.

He continued to press forward until the swell of her bottom was cradled by his pelvis. Even though he'd made her wear a butt plug, his cock was far larger and stretched her far more. He groaned as he seated himself in her ass and then began to move inside her.

Roark thrust gently. The movement was far different from the normally powerful stroking she'd become used to. He seemed more intent on savoring her response, allowing her back passage to accept and enjoy this new carnal pleasure, than in achieving his own release. She couldn't help but think that her dark rosebud had to be strangling his large staff... and she didn't care. The new sensations were wickedly exquisite.

She hadn't expected to enjoy it. She had thought he would force her to endure, but he seemed intent instead in making her crave his touch in this way as well. Slowly, but surely, the sting from his first breaching gave way to a profound sense of submissiveness that only enhanced her pleasure. Sage had never expected to enjoy having her ass fucked, and certainly never thought to need it, but she was wrong.

Sage's beaded nipples ached, her clit throbbed, and her pussy pulsed in the same tempo as he stroked her back passage. Her body was alight with arousal and need, just as it was when he fucked her pussy. Sage's sighs morphed into a deep keening as he drove into her again and again. She clutched and grasped at the bedclothes, desperate for something to do with her hands.

"Roark," she wailed. Every muscle in her body convulsed as the neurons fired, sending wave after wave of pleasure to wash over her. Her darkest channel clamped down on his plunging rod and Roark groaned in response.

"Come for me. Show me you're sorry for disobeying me, and you want me to use whichever hole I want, whenever I want." She moaned in surrender and need. "That's my good girl."

The tempo and speed with which Roark moved inside her increased; his cock began to thicken as he began to spend himself. The pumping of his seed triggered an automatic response, and she came, her dark sheath clamping down on him rhythmically. When at last he was done, he leaned over her back, kissing and nuzzling her to ease her return from her rapturous flight. When she sighed and relaxed beneath him, he followed her down and then eased himself from her body. Never during the entire interlude was he ever in danger of losing control.

He lifted her in his arms and strode into the bath. Adjusting the water temp and pressure of the wondrous shower, he stepped in and placed her on her feet, careful to ensure she was leaning against him so he could support her weight. He washed her gently, interspersing his bathing with kisses and caresses until her body was languid in his embrace. Carrying her back to their bed, after drying her gently, he tucked her in, then leaned down to kiss her. When he started to move away, she reached out to catch his hand. He smiled, returning to kiss her again.

"I'm just going to get my laptop, love. I'm not going anywhere."

Sage waited until he returned and propped himself up in bed, then using his leg as a kind of body pillow, she cradled her head in his lap and was asleep almost instantly.

∽

Sage woke, wrapped in Roark's embrace. She feared one morning she would wake, and he'd be trapped again inside the pages of her novel.

"Didn't you hear me tell you I wasn't going to leave you?" he whispered. "Whatever it was that pulled me out of the book isn't strong enough to force me back."

"You don't know that."

"I do. I've been trying to break free… to pierce the veil, as it were. Each time, it felt as though I got closer. When I realized you were in danger, no power that ever existed was going to be strong enough to contain me. I broke free and came for you. Therefore, there isn't anything that could trap me again. Makes sense, right?"

She nodded, agreeing with him. It did have a certain kind of logic. The ass fucking he'd given her the night before had not been the last time he'd had his way with her. She'd vowed never to write that in a novel, but now understood the reality of that scenario. She was stiff, sore, and happier than she had ever been in her life. Roark sat up, and Sage snuggled against him.

"Did you find anything?" she asked.

"I did. Or, more accurately, I was able to unravel a motive for someone to want to kill you. Our friend, Eddy, was able to trace the source of funding from your Mr. Shackelford back to the person who hired him."

"You know? Then can we have Holmes…?"

"That was one of your more obnoxious name choices." He grinned. "But yes, Michael should be able to help us. The problem is what we have as proof would never be admissible. He isn't unsympathetic, and like in the books, he basically told me he'd look the other way if I wanted to handle the situation, but for the Yard to arrest her and put her away…"

"Her?" Sage interrupted.

He nodded slowly, his eyes never leaving her face.

"Gail?"

"Yes, love. I rather suspect she's been behind all of it—the attempts in North Carolina and the threatening note here. That way, when you ended up dead, it would just be seen as part of the pattern of a crazed stalker. She's been embezzling from you for years—underreporting sales, overreporting expenses. It's a mess. So, we have the motive, know what she did and who she hired, we just need to connect the dots. I went back and read all those emails and reexamined your royalty reports. It became obvious your publisher was a bully and was embezzling money—and not just from you. Those emails from her after you left are pretty damning, but they won't hold up in court."

"What if I confront her wearing a wire?"

"No… that's far too dangerous. At this point, she'll be like a cornered, wounded animal…"

"I'll have you, Gabe, and Michael for backup, and she won't expect me to have the spine to do anything, even if I confront her."

He shook his head. "You will have showed her your hand, exposed yourself, and she still might not implicate herself."

"If she doesn't say anything, at least she knows that I know. Then if you and Holmes step out, she'll know you know, which should freak her out. Come on, Roark…"

"Do you remember how gently I fucked your bottom hole last night?" he growled.

She nodded.

"If you disobey me and put yourself in danger, *that* will become a fond memory. I won't be nearly as gentle when I fuck your ass after I've welted it for you first. Do you hear me, Sage?"

"But if we…"

"Again, with the 'we.' There is no 'we' in this situation. You will stay safe, and Michael and I will deal with Ms. Vincent."

"But…"

"Precisely. It will be your butt that pays the price for your disobedience." He looked down at her, silently daring her to continue arguing with him. Try as she might, Sage just couldn't hold his stare.

Dropping her eyes, she said morosely, "I just wanted to help. And I am the one she tried to kill."

Roark pulled her into his embrace, stroking her body until all the tension left and she melted into him.

"I know, love. That's why I don't want you involved. I couldn't stand it if something happened to you. We'll make sure she pays… one way or another."

Sage saw the soft, loving look fade from his eyes to be replaced by a distant coldness that made her shiver.

"I'm sorry I ever wrote that ending. I never saw

you as a killer, just a man with his back against the wall with no good choices."

In one of her latest novels, Roark had killed an unarmed man in cold blood. Granted, the guy deserved to die, but some readers had been taken aback.

"Don't fret." Roark hugged her. "He needed to die, and I'm the one who needed to kill him. It was a brave choice for you to make."

CHAPTER 11

For the next few days, Roark ensured Sage was far too occupied with starting a new series, hiring a public relations firm, meeting with Scotland Yard, and allowing herself to fall deeply, madly in love with him. Truth to tell, that last part hadn't been difficult. She was beginning to believe he was right—he'd always been her own romantic hero, but she hadn't seen him as a Dom. She hadn't seen that he was exactly what she needed, even when she didn't want to follow the rules.

Holmes had escorted Roark to file a writ or some kind of legal document to force Gail to open her books and her Swiss accounts to a criminal forensic accountant. Sage hadn't even known she had one Swiss account, not to mention several.

The hotel phone rang.

"Sage Matthews."

"Sage, darling, it's Gail. I ended up extending my stay. I feel bad about the way things ended between us, and I think maybe we both said some things that we perhaps regret…"

Gail continued to prattle on, but Sage wasn't really listening. She wanted to tell her that she had proof of her embezzlement, knew Gail had tried to kill her, and Roark was filing the necessary paperwork to see her pay for what she'd done. Then Gail said something interesting.

"I really think we ought to have lunch and part as friends."

Friends? But if she wanted to meet, maybe she could show Roark she wasn't as helpless as he sometimes seemed to think she was. If she was going to make a life with him, he needed to know she was a competent individual and could help him in his work… between writing her new series.

So, instead of telling her to fuck off, she said, "I'd like that, Gail. I agree we meant too much to each other over the years. Can you do it today, here at the Savoy?"

Gail laughed. How had she never heard that bitter note of winter in Gail's voice?

"I heard you had moved into the Savoy as a writer-in-residence. And how clever of your new PR firm to come up with the idea of getting some uber-sexy model to portray your lover and muse, your inspiration for Clive Thomas as it were. Finally going to retire that series?"

Sage was still having trouble accepting that Roark's character in the books had now been replaced by a character named Clive Thomas. It was curious. Only she and the characters that had stepped out of her novels knew that any substitution had been made.

"Yes, I thought I'd give him his own happily-ever-after with a feisty heroine, the kind you always hated. Say one o'clock this afternoon? I'll make a reservation."

"Lovely. See you then."

Shaking her head, she dialed Roark's cell. They both continued to marvel at the fact everything she'd ever written about Roark—money, fashion, virility, etc.—had come with him from the novels. The only thing that hadn't been in her books was his Dom-ness.

"What's up, love?" he answered. "We're with the Crown Prosecutors."

"When will you be home?"

"Put your motor on idle, sweetheart. I will take care of you when I get back there. Be a good girl and follow the rules. We don't want a repeat of yesterday's lesson, do we?"

Before she had a chance to say anything, he disconnected. She started to get angry and call him back, then remembered her phone had a record feature. She and Gail would be in the Savoy, for God's sake. She could let Felix and Gabe know she was having lunch with her nemesis. Besides which, what could possibly happen at the Savoy?

Sage took a shower and dressed with care. She put on a pair of black leather trousers with ankle boots. She paired it with a black leather corset and an eggplant-colored, raw silk swing coat. She wanted to meet her adversary on equal footing. At precisely one, she left her room. Gail could bloody well wait for her for a change. Hanging back until she saw Gail enter the restaurant, Sage straightened her spine, turned on the recorder, and headed to the table. She had specifically asked for a very public table by the window.

"Sage, darling, it's not like you to be late."

"I find these days I'm so busy, I can only be on time for the really important things… and people."

"Well done," Gail said with a sly smile. "I see your new firm got you into some decent clothes."

"Actually, it was Roark. He knows several of the London designers, and they were happy to send his woman some things. We're attending a big art thing next week, and the gowns I had to choose from were simply stunning."

Gail looked taken aback for a moment but quickly recovered.

"I felt bad about some things I said and frankly,

about not listening to you when you wanted to start your little paranormal series. I know that isn't usually something I do, but I feel I should have made an exception for your vanity project. I know you can't have a publisher yet, so I thought maybe we should meet and put all this unpleasantness behind us. As you said, we've meant a lot to each other over the years."

"My vanity project? Hardly. I do find it curious, for once, your information from the gossips is behind the times. I do, in fact, have a new publisher. We only recently inked the deal, but it is a very lucrative one. I stand to make so much more money than I ever did with you. They're very excited, the writing is going really well, and I should have the manuscript to them by the end of the month."

"Really?" Gail couldn't quite mask her surprise fast enough. "Well… good for you. For what it must be costing you to stay here and pay that model, you'll need the money. Then why, I wonder, did you agree to meet? Wanting to gloat? That's not like you."

"You don't know the first thing about what makes me tick. And no, I have no need to gloat, and Roark is not a cover model. He's my lover and my Dom. I've moved into his permanent suite here at the Savoy. The funny thing is, I used his suite for my inspiration for Clive's suite. It's curious how art often imitates life. I just wanted to tell you how wonderful things are going, and I know you hired William Shackelford to kill me. I can't prove it yet, but Roark and DSI Holmes at Scotland Yard are working on it." Sage let that sink in before standing and motioning to the maître d'.

"See that anything Ms. Vincent wants is put on our account. Kiss-kiss, Gail. Enjoy yourself. I doubt you have many more days of freedom or much money left."

Sage spun on her heel and headed back for the lift, hearing Gail scrambling to extricate herself from the table. Gail caught up with her just before the lift doors opened.

"You bitch," Gail seethed. "I made you. You were nothing before I found you, and you'll be nothing after this new book of yours bombs. But it won't matter," she said, lowering her voice and leaning close to Sage, "because you'll be dead."

Gail pulled a hatpin from her stylish vintage veiled pillbox hat and swung it in an arc toward Sage, who jumped back and crashed into something very large and very solid… Roark knocked the hatpin from Gail's hands. Sage made a wild dive for it before it fell down the shaft of the lift as the door opened. Grasping it by the pearlized end, she held it aloft and looked at Roark triumphantly, but his dark eyes held Satan's own fury. She wanted desperately to believe it was directed toward Gail, but her butt clenched. She knew full well who would feel the sting of his displeasure.

"Really, Gail?" she said, ignoring her growing arousal. "I had the villainess in The Toxic Corpse try to kill Clive with a poisoned hatpin." Sage fished around in the large pockets of her swing coat and produced two plastic baggies, dropping her phone into one and the hatpin into the other, then turned back to Roark.

"If you give this to DSI Holmes, I'll bet he finds traces of thallium," Sage said, handing both baggies to Roark. "And I had my phone set to record."

Gail seemed dumbstruck for an instant before turning around to make a hasty retreat. Only she ran into something rather large and solid—Gabriel Watson.

Roark extended the baggies with the hatpin and Sage's phone to Felix, who had arrived with Gabe. Gabe had apprehended Gail, and she was unable to get away.

"Handle this carefully," Roark said, "and give it to DSI Holmes. According to Nancy Drew here, it's coated in a lethal poison, and the other has some fairly damning evidence."

"Very good, sir," Felix said.

"I'll take care of ensuring Ms. Vincent is handed over to the Yard," Gabe said as he removed a hissing and spitting Gail from the lobby into his office, where she could be held without disturbing the Savoy's patrons.

Roark turned to Sage, pulling her into his embrace. "Room, corner, strip, now," he whispered before his mouth crashed down on hers in a fiery kiss. "I need to speak to Gabe and Felix, but you had better be waiting for me when I get there."

"Yes, Sir," she answered softly and meekly.

Sage went back to their room and did as instructed. She didn't have long to wait before the door opened and Roark entered the room.

"Of all the lame, foolish, reckless stunts. What do you have to say for yourself? No, wait, it doesn't matter. All I need to know is… did you really think if you'd told me what you were planning to do, I'd have given you permission? You couldn't have possibly thought that since you didn't have my permission to leave our room," he thundered.

"But I got the evidence of what she was doing! I recorded her trying to kill me. She was apprehended with the murder weapon in her hand," she said, whirling around to face him.

"Do you bloody think I give a damn about that? She could have killed you!"

Sage stared in horrified fascination as Roark unbuttoned his cuffs and rolled up his sleeves before unbuckling his belt.

"You put your nose in that corner, Sage. Hands against the wall, bottom pushed out, legs spread."

"Roark?" she barely managed to squeak out.

"That's the third time you've risked your life and the second time you've left our room without my permission. Obviously, a mere spanking, followed by a rough fucking, isn't getting through to you. Let's see if a set of welts makes an impression."

"Welts? Now? With no warmup? Is that even allowed?" she said in a rush, starting to panic.

"I don't have to do anything I don't want to, and you haven't behaved well enough to be eased into a welting. Now, Sage," he growled the last.

She turned back to the corner and complied. The only warning she had that she was about to get her first taste of a belt applied to her backside was a *swoosh* a fraction of a second before his belt laid a two-inch lick of fire across her bottom. Sage wailed and bounced up on her toes, trying to tuck her tail. The strap of hellfire struck again, intersecting with the first weal.

"No, Sage, push that bottom back out. I intend your first welting to be memorable. You will *not* put yourself in danger!"

It was the desperation in his voice that stole her breath and will away. It was obvious he was at a loss how to ensure her safety, and as he'd said, he meant to make this bad enough she never tempted fate again. If he'd yelled at her, it would have been easier, but knowing she had scared him did more damage than the belt ever would. She caved in and began sobbing.

The third strike was even worse, landing across the lower part of her backside and intersecting with both he'd already laid down. She bit back a scream, the fire and searing agony beyond anything she'd ever experienced.

"Roark, Master, please, I'm sorry. I'll behave," she cried.

It seemed in times of extreme emotion, the honorarium came easily and naturally.

"You're damn right, you'll behave."

She sagged against the wall a complete mess—sobbing, sniffling, mascara running, snot dribbling out of her nose. Sage heard his belt slice through the air a fourth time.

"You're doing very well, love. I'm proud of you… angry but proud." His tone softened as she collapsed against the wall. "Do you think you can take one more?"

That did it—Sage completely lost it. Reluctantly, she nodded and remained facing the corner, her hands braced against the wall, pushing her bottom out to embrace one last strapping. She might have thought she was ready, but when it landed, it still drove her back onto her tiptoes, where she bounced, trying to lessen the agony… and failing. She tried sucking and gasping air, but that didn't help either.

"That's my good girl," he crooned lovingly.

Sage was a study in abject misery. Her bottom was swollen, with raw weals of fire splayed across it. She rested her head on the wall, crying hot, silent tears.

The worst part wasn't the pain but the desire clawing at her insides, causing her nipples to bead and her pussy to pool its wet heat. Her sheath had clenched as each welt landed and now was rhythmically spasming in anticipation. Instead of enfolding her in his embrace, he pressed her upper body into the wall and rained a fury of blistering swats all across her backside, which wouldn't have been half as painful were it not for landing on the fresh weals.

"No..." she wailed.

The pain was beyond excruciating, but worse than the physical pain was the fact she was wildly aroused and an emotional disaster. She didn't care how much she hurt—all she wanted was to feel Roark's cock surging into her, pounding her pussy into the same level of submission he'd just beat into her ass. Reaching between her legs, he chuckled, finding the evidence of her shameful need.

Sage would always recall that was the exact moment she realized she had capitulated to him completely—mentally, emotionally, physically, and sexually. Roark's fingers played lightly across the weals he'd given her. Her body shuddered, and she feared she would collapse in a puddle of gooey need at his feet.

"I know more than one way to make you sore, Sage," he said, "but that's going to have to wait."

"Wait?" she asked incredulously.

"When you misbehave to the point I have to take my belt to your beautiful backside, I'm not necessarily going to ease your need to be forgiven and fucked. While you are most definitely forgiven, that need for a sexual release that's surging through your system will have to wait. Go wash your face and fix your makeup. We have an appointment at Dark Garden."

"Roark…"

"What do you call me when you're being punished?"

"Master. I'm sorry, but please don't make me put on those leather pants… please?"

"Hmm, I ought to, but those weals are coming up nicely. Why don't you put on the little black dress with the deep asymmetrical neckline, black bra, and black stockings." He glanced at his watch. "Hurry along, love. I don't want to be late."

She realized saying no was not an option. She slipped into the bathroom, fixed her face, and came back out to get dressed. He opened the drawer and pulled out his favorite butt plug and a pocket rocket with a remote control. He looked up and grinned.

She was fairly sure he could read her expression of concern as he slipped each into his pocket.

"Just in case my girl needs to be reprimanded while we're out."

She only barely kept herself from rolling her eyes. Once dressed, Roark escorted her downstairs and to a waiting town car. She was a bit surprised to see a pillow on the back seat and blushed when she realized Roark must have arranged for it. She wasn't sure if she should be angry, humiliated, or grateful for his doing so.

"Do you know the Dark Garden?" asked Roark, after helping her in, joining her, and closing the door.

"Yes, sir, I do indeed." The driver's eyes caught Sage's in the rearview mirror. "My missus would love to go there, but it's a bit too rich for my blood."

They pulled up to a beautiful Georgian building with a discreet sign. Roark paid the driver whose eyes lit up when he saw the size of the tip.

"Thank you, sir!" he gasped.

"Every man should be able to treat his lady in the manner she deserves. I believe there should be enough there for an intimate meal at the Savoy as well. When you call, tell them to give you my table."

They exited the town car, Sage waiting for Roark to help her out. The owner, Louis, came out to greet them and escorted them inside.

"Roark, how very nice to see you, *mon ami*. Is this your beautiful Sage?"

"It is. Sage this is Louis, he's been making exquisite lingerie for the longest time. Louis, I want to get Sage some new things. Except for this morning, she has been a very good girl."

Sage whirled and looked at him. "You can't expect me to strip down for a fitting?"

"Why ever not? I'm quite sure Louis has seen more than one submissive's backside showing the evidence of her Dom's disapproval and discipline."

"I have indeed. You are not to concern yourself. Roark, do you know what you're looking for?"

"Roark…" she pleaded.

"Sage, do I need to ask Louis for some privacy?"

She searched his face and saw nothing there that said he'd back down or not carry through on the veiled threat to insert either the butt plug, the mini-vibrator, or both.

"No, Sir."

"Good girl," he said, hugging her and kissing her temple. "What I'd like is for a complete set of measurements to be taken. Then I'd like to see what you have on hand that can be customized as well as some fabrics for some completely custom things. I'm afraid Sage doesn't have much in the way of lingerie that I care for."

"Do you want matching bottoms?" asked Louis solicitously.

"Only a few, and I'll let you know which ones."

"This way, *mademoiselle*," Louis said, indicating a back area. "There is no one here, Roark, so the room adjacent to the back garden is available. I have a few things that should work for her, but I'll have my assistant bring you samples of the fabrics we have available."

"Thank you, Louis. Run along, Sage, and be a good girl."

Sage found herself ushered into the back where Louis waited for her to disrobe.

"Can't we do this with my clothes on?" she asked.

"No, the measurements would not be accurate. Roark is a very exacting man and I rather imagine he will not be happy if I have to tell him you were uncooperative."

Sage sighed and turned her back so Louis could unzip the dress. She slipped it off her shoulders and let it pool on the floor at her feet. Louis leaned down to help her out of her shoes and stockings so that she was completely naked.

"You must have angered Roark something fierce to have earned a welting such as that. I should be able to make this fairly painless for you."

"Thank you. I suppose I did."

"Arms up," he said as he brought out a lovely

hand-embroidered corset that he quickly had her laced into. "This one does come with a matching thong, but I'm sure it will fit. Let's go show this one to Roark."

He led her to a comfortable salon-like area that opened off an impressive formal garden. Roark looked up from the fabric samples and smiled. It wasn't the indulgent, loving smile, of her lover. It was far more predatory and feral than that and jump-started her arousal.

She suddenly wanted him to be very proud of her and wanted to acknowledge her submission in a way that both he and Louis would understand. She crossed the distance between them and sank gracefully to her knees—thighs spread wide, hands palms up, and her head bowed. She'd never knelt for any man. While she acknowledged that she had a deep need to be submissive during sex, she'd never truly submitted to anyone… until now.

Sage saw the toes of his loafers come into sight as his fingertips stroked her head.

"Is she not the most beautiful thing you've ever seen, Louis?"

"She is indeed. The gift of a woman's submission is a thing to be cherished. That she chooses to show you that submission in front of someone else, outside of a club, is rare."

"My Sage is like no other. I am humbled and proud to be her Dom."

"As you should be," said Louis.

Sage glanced up at him and took the hand he extended to her to help her up.

"Have you ever knelt for anyone?" he asked softly.

"Never. Not even when playing at a club. I…" she faltered. She knew what she felt for Roark, but he'd never said the L word to her… never even mentioned it.

He smiled benignly. "I love you, too, sweetheart. I have loved you long before that fateful night by the bridge, and I should have told you long before now. I apologize. Will you forgive me?"

Sage threw her arms around him. "Always," she whispered, drawing his head down to hers.

His kiss was long and sensual, his tongue playing across the seam of her mouth as it opened to his and it surged in—tasting, savoring, gently dominating. One of his hands twisted in her hair, tilting her head back, lighting up her scalp and firing all of the neurons in her system. The other hand stroked down her back and deftly traced one of her welts before gently cupping her ass. Oh lord, she was going to have to get out of this corset with stiffened nipples.

As if reading her mind, he whispered in her ear. "It won't just be your nipples, sweetheart, he'll be able to see and smell your arousal."

Roark trailed his finger from the underside of

her ass around to the front of her mons, slipping it between her legs to tickle her clit before giving it a wicked pinch.

"Ouch! What was that for?"

"For not responding appropriately."

"I'm so sorry, Roark. I love you, too. Forgive me?"

"Always."

They turned when they heard a discreet snuffle from behind them.

"I'm sorry. It always touches my romantic soul to see a couple so in love with one another."

The rest of the fitting was enjoyable as Sage realized that Louis had most likely seen many women in various stages of having been punished and aroused by their partners. Louis had two more corsets that he could customize to Sage's figure, and then Roark ordered three more.

Sage started to protest when she saw the size of the bill, but that protest was cut off with a sharp swat to her backside.

"Don't you remember you wrote me as fabulously wealthy? And I know how much money you have."

Sage grinned. "We have. I want us to share everything."

Roark had paid the town car and driver to wait. He helped her into the car, drawing the curtain between the front and back sections as he climbed in. He sat next to her and she realized she hadn't been the only one who was aroused by their trip to Dark Garden.

His eyes never leaving hers, he reached down and unbuckled his belt before unbuttoning his fly and reaching in to pull his cock out. It stood up, completely engorged and jutting straight out from his body. He tugged her off the back seat and Sage started to sink to her knees again so she could suck his cock. Linking his hands with hers, he stopped her and pushed up the sides of her dress.

"It's not your mouth I want, sweetheart."

He gave her a gentle tug, directing her legs to either side of his body, then slowly lowered her onto his cock. Her pussy was more than ready to receive his large, hard staff. It slipped in easily, filling her and making her moan just from the act of penetrating her. He directed her hands to his shoulders and then spanned her waist with his own.

"Roark," she groaned.

"Good girl. God, you feel good." His voice had taken on the dark, rich notes she identified as those that accompanied only his deepest arousal.

Gravity was her friend as she lowered herself completely, seating his cock deep inside her. She moaned, her head falling backwards as a mini orgasm washed over her, her sheath contracting all along his length. When her pussy relaxed, he surged up with his hips and she cried out.

He began thrusting in and out of her, holding her in place. Even now, when she was, for all intents and purposes, on top, he was still in control. He began to fuck her with a rhythm that was strong and sure. She writhed on top of him, trying to take him deeper and allowing her lust to soar.

Roark allowed her a little movement and they easily found their rhythm as she balanced on his shoulders and he began hammering her pussy. Her second orgasm sparked and spread like wildfire, coursing through her system and leaving her breathless. He took two more strokes before he grasped her hips, grinding her down on his groin as he began spilling himself into her.

When he'd finished, he cupped the nape of her neck and brought her mouth to his as he kissed her deeply. He helped her off his lap and tucked himself back into his jeans before straightening her dress. They had barely finished before they returned to the Savoy.

Roark waited until they were in the elevator before swinging her up in his arms and carrying her to their room. He opened the door and took her into the room.

"You go get naked, love." He glanced at his watch. "Dinner should be delivered in just a few minutes."

"I suppose I'm going to be naked for dinner and you aren't?"

Roark kissed her. "Such a smart girl. You have an excellent grasp of the situation."

She heard the discreet knock as room service delivered and set up their meal. When she heard them leave, she left the privacy of the bath.

"Any chance I could have a robe or one of your shirts?"

"None at all," he answered.

"Why is there only one chair?" she asked.

"Because you're going to sit in my lap and feed me."

She grinned. She hadn't written Roark to be this sensual and romantic, but she was glad that he had enhanced and expanded upon all of her fantasies—both those she'd written and those she'd only imagined. Sage made herself comfortable and lifted the cloche off the dish closest to her as she began to feed him. He'd ensured that they didn't need utensils, but that there were sauces for him to lick and suck from her fingers.

Sage should have been embarrassed as her nectar began to leak onto his jeans, but she wasn't. She'd come to thoroughly enjoy the feelings of arousal and how sexy he made her feel with little effort on his part. When she reached for the final cover that concealed dessert, he lightly swatted her hand and shook his head. Sage put her hands back in her lap and leaned into his body, resting her head on his shoulder.

Roark reached around her and pulled the lid off the last covered dish. It wasn't the gorgeous confection that was revealed that made her gasp, it was what sat in the middle of it—a ring with a large center stone brilliant in cut, carat, and color. She grinned like a Cheshire cat. She had described this ring in perfect detail as having once belonged to his mother.

Roark didn't say a word, just slipped it on her ring finger and then began to feed her the decadent dessert. When they were finished, he stood up and carried her to their bed, laying her gently and reverently on her back.

Following her down, he said, "I plan to spend the rest of my life making good on the promise of that."

Sage was never sure if that was a threat or a promise and found she didn't care. When she woke the next morning still wrapped in his arms, she was filled with a joy that could only be favorably compared to a child waking up on Christmas morning, waiting to go downstairs to open presents, anticipating the bright future that lay before her. Stretching, she noticed the dazzling sparkle on her left hand.

"I'd better be long dead, buried, and turned into worm food before you take it off," he rumbled at her, nuzzling her neck. "Understand?"

"Yes, Sir," she purred, snuggling against him,

thinking how very nice it was to have found her very own happy ending.

∼

Dying to know what happens next? Turn the page for a First Look into NEGOTIATION the next book in the series.

FIRST LOOK

NEGOTIATION

Rachel Moriarty? Had Sage enlisted one of the constable's help in making a joke? Perhaps he should speak to Roark about her penchant for making jokes of people's names.

As he rounded the corner and spied her sitting there, he had to admit if she was one of Sage's creations, he'd have to rethink asking Roark to scold her. Rachel Moriarty was gorgeous—she looked to be a bit taller than average with light brown hair streaked with silver and highlights from the sun. He couldn't tell exactly from where he was standing, but she looked to have a curvaceous figure that she tried to hide in dumpy clothes.

He idly wondered what she'd look like in a corset and G-string, no boy shorts, at Baker Street, the BDSM club he'd begun frequenting. It allowed him to exert control and dominance in sexual manners, meet his own needs, and help submissives with theirs. And all done with a contract in place protecting both him and the submissive he was playing with. Actually, almost anonymous sex had seemed ideal when he'd been introduced to the club, but the more time he was out of Sage's books, the more he longed for the kind of true connection, Roark had found with Sage—a kind of private intimacy they could take out into the world and not just leave behind in the bedroom or when they were playing.

"Ms. Moriarty? I'm DSI Michael Holmes. The constable seemed to think you were in some distress and that I might be able to help."

"Actually…"

So, she was American.

"It's Dr. Moriarty. And did you say Holmes?"

Michael chuckled. "Yes, a rather unfortunate name for a detective…"

She picked up the large purse that had been sitting beside her. "And people think the English don't have a sense of humor. I hope your constable is having a good laugh…"

Michael reached out to grasp her elbow lightly. "I won't tell you I don't think Landry spoke to me because of the names, but I can assure you I am a DSI and if you have a problem, I'd like to help."

She glanced around furtively, seemed to think about it, and then nodded. "I promise you this is not a joke on my part."

"How long have you been visiting us here in England?"

"What makes you think I'm not a citizen?" she challenged, bringing her chin up a notch.

So, the girl had spirit—dreadful taste in clothing—but she was feisty.

She shook her head. "The accent. My apologies DSI Holmes, it seems my nerves are getting the better of me and I'm lashing out."

He chuckled. "I assure you, Dr. Moriarty, that if that is your idea of lashing out, you and I should get along famously. Why don't we into one of the privacy rooms." He escorted her down a short hall and into a private waiting room. He held out a chair and noticed how gracefully she sank into it. *Would she have that kind of grace sinking to her knees? God, he really needed to make time to get to Baker Street.* "Now, what brings you to Scotland Yard?"

"You're going to think I'm crazy, but I assure you I'm not."

"Go on," he urged gently.

"I hold a PhD in English History, specializing in the War of the Roses through the reign of Elizabeth I. Five years ago, I relocated to London and began my business, Select Tours. I specialize in small, private tours catered to an individual or small group's specific interests."

"I've heard good things about your company. I have friends at the Savoy and they speak well of you."

"You have? Your accent pegs you as born and raised in London, the West End if I'm not mistaken."

"You have an ear for accents. Not far from Leicester Square. A few months ago, you took a friend of mine on a tour she still raves about—Sage Matthews."

"The author? Lovely person. So kind and unassuming. I didn't know what to expect when I met her. Her husband seems quite intimidating…"

"But madly in love with Sage. Roark and I have been friends for years. I've never known him to be as happy and settled as he is now."

Her body was tense and he wondered if a session with a caring Dom might be just what she need to quiet what was an obviously busy mind.

"Yes, they did seem to have a very intimate and loving connection…" Her mind seemed to have drifted away with her sentence.

"But I don't suppose you came here to talk about the Savoy's most illustrious couple."

"No. No, I didn't. You're going to think I'm crazy…"

"I assure you I won't."

She nodded again. "I was in Whitechapel, conducting a tour after dark. We were in the actual flat where Mary Jane Kelly met her end…"

"I didn't know they allowed people up there."

She smiled. It transformed her face even though the smile did not reach her eyes.

"Because I keep my number so small and I have a doctorate in English history…"

"But Jack the Ripper operated in the time of Queen Victoria, long after Elizabeth the First."

"Yes, but it fascinates people to this day and the beauty of what I offer is I can cater my tours to the client."

He nodded. "I'm sorry. Please, go on."

"We were headed down to the street level when I noticed the door to her room was slightly ajar. I was certain I had locked it, but I went back to do so. As I grasped the knob, I felt someone pulling on it from the other side—someone strong. When it was about halfway open, I heard a woman scream and then it felt as if a powerful force passed through my body… For the past several nights, I've awakened in my loft. The door to my balcony has been open, even though I know for certain I closed and locked it. And there's an icy chill in the flat… This was a mistake. I'm sure you think…"

"What I think, Dr. Moriarty, is that you are frightened and in need of help. I'm not sure that I can do anything officially, I think perhaps you and I should call Roark and Sage and have Roark treat us to lunch at the Savoy."

"I couldn't possibly presume…"

Michael grinned at her. "Maybe not, but that's what old friends are for. Besides, he's loaded, and the Savoy has an exceptional menu."

Do you think you know what happens? Read NEGOTIATION to find out.

Other books in the series
Advance
Negotiation
Submission
Contract
Bound

Interested in the stories about wolf shifters that Sage wants to write? They already exist! You can read about them in the Wayward Mates and the Tangled Vines series. You can read all about them on my website www.deltajames.com

Thank you for reading *Advance!* I hope you loved it.

Sign up for my newsletter https://www.subscribepage.com/VIPlist22019 and get access to free books, plus you will hear about sales, exclusive previews and new releases first.

If you enjoyed this book I would love if you left a review, they make a huge difference for indie authors.

As always, my thanks to all of you for reading my books.

Take care of yourselves and each other.

ABOUT THE AUTHOR

Other books by Delta James: https://www.deltajames.com/

If you're looking for paranormal or contemporary erotic romance, you've found your new favorite author!

Alpha heroes find real love with feisty heroines in Delta James' sinfully sultry romances. Welcome to a world where true love conquers all and good triumphs over evil! Delta's stories are filled with erotic encounters of romance and discipline.

∽

If you're on Facebook, please join my closed group, Delta's Wayward Pack! Don't miss out on the giveaways, early teasers and hot men!
https://www.facebook.com/groups/348982795738444

ALSO BY DELTA JAMES

Masters of the Savoy

Advance - https://books2read.com/advance

Negotiation – https://books2read.com/negotiate

Submission - https://books2read.com/submission1

Contract – https://books2read.com/contract1

Bound – https://books2read.com/bound3

Fated Legacy

Touch of Fate - https://books2read.com/legacytof

Touch of Darkness - https://books2read.com/legacytod

Touch of Light – https://books2read.com/legacytol

Touch of Fire – https://books2read.com/legacyfire

Touch of Ice – https://books2read.com/legacytoi

Touch of Destiny – https://books2read.com/legacydestiny

Syndicate Masters

The Bargain - https://books2read.com/thebargain

Masters of the Deep

Silent Predator - https://

books2read.com/silentpredator

Fierce Predator – https://books2read.com/Fiercepredator

Ghost Cat Canyon

Determined - https://books2read.com/ghostcatdetermined

Untamed - https://books2read.com/ghostcatuntamed

Bold - https://books2read.com/ghostcatbold

Fearless - https://books2read.com/ghostcatfearless

Strong - https://books2read.com/ghostcatstrong

Boxset - https://books2read.com/Ghostcatset

Tangled Vines

Corked – https://books2read.com/corked1

Uncorked - https://books2read.com/uncorked

Decanted - https://books2read.com/decanted

Breathe - https://books2read.com/breathe1

Full Bodied - https://books2read.com/fullbodied

Late Harvest - https://books2read.com/lateharvest

Boxset 1 – https://books2read.com/TVbox1

Boxset 2 – https://books2read.com/Tvbox2

Mulled Wine – https://books2read.com/mulledwine

Wild Mustang

Hampton - https://books2read.com/hamptonw

Mac - https://books2read.com/macw

Croft – https://books2read.com/newcroft-dj

Noah - https://books2read.com/newnoah-dj

Thom - https://books2read.com/newthom-dj

Reid - https://books2read.com/newreid-dj

Wayward Mates

Brought to Heel: https://books2read.com/u/m0w9P7

Marked and Mated: https://books2read.com/u/4DRNpO

Mastering His Mate: https://books2read.com/u/bxaYE6

Taking His Mate: https://books2read.com/u/4joarZ

Claimed and Mated: https://books2read.com/u/bPxorY

Claimed and Mastered: https://books2read.com/u/3LRvM0

Hunted and Claimed: https://books2read.com/u/bPQZ6d

Captured and Claimed: https://books2read.com/u/4A5Jk0